# Abba,
## give me
## a word

the path of spiritual direction

L. Roger Owens

PARACLETE PRESS

BREWSTER, MASSACHUSETTS

*Abba, Give Me a Word: The Path of Spiritual Direction*

2012 First Printing

ISBN 978-1-55725-799-4

Library of Congress Cataloging-in-Publication Data
Owens, L. Roger, 1975-
  Abba, give me a word : the path of spiritual direction / L. Roger Owens.
     p. cm.
  Includes bibliographical references (p.       ).
  ISBN 978-1-55725-799-4 (trade pbk.)
  1. Spiritual direction—Christianity.  I. Title.
  BV5053.O94 2012
  253.5'3—dc23                                      2011051650


        10 9 8 7 6 5 4 3 2 1

Published by Paraclete Press
Brewster, Massachusetts
www.paracletepress.com

Printed in the United States of America

For my father, Max Owens

(1920–2009)

# Contents

# My Father's House

I make the drive every month. I've been doing it for five years. It used to be only five miles, now it's forty-seven. It's still worth it.

I get in my station wagon after lunch, put a Diet Rite in the cupholder, and toss an apple in the passenger seat for the trip home. I back out of the driveway and away from all the things I have left inside the house—task lists, briefcase, half-written sermon, as many worries as I can. I leave my wife, Ginger, with whom I just had lunch, after I tell her that I will be back in time to pick up the boys from school.

I drive a mile and a half to get out of the subdivision, then onto the bypass, then onto the interstate. Finally I feel as if I'm on my way.

It takes a while to get out of Durham, North Carolina, since the limits of this city of nearly 230,000 seem to expand farther every day. But in fifteen minutes I pass over Falls Lake, and then my mind begins to quiet from all I have left behind. Crossing the bridge feels like a point of transition for me because when I see the ospreys and the bald eagles, I am reminded of why I'm doing this—to become like the ones the prophet Isaiah talked about, who wait on the Lord and mount up with wings as eagles, and run and run and never tire.

Just past the lake, I turn off the interstate and onto country roads and through towns that even sound rural: Butner, Franklinton, and, finally, Louisburg. Louisburg, the Franklin county seat, with a population of 3,000, has one grocery store worth going to, a small coffee shop and bookstore called the Coffee Hound where the people in town who like books can connect, and a couple of boutique shops that are closed every Monday. There's a declining two-year college in town, a monument to the Confederate dead, and a plain brown office building on Church Street with a parking lot across the street.

That's where I always park.

The sign on the brown building next to the door tells me that I can find an appraiser and a lawyer inside, neither of whom I see very often. The sign outside doesn't say anything about the office at the end of the hallway, the one with a navy blue sofa and a candle already lit, with the bookshelves full of Bible commentaries and books on prayer, and contemplative music playing. The sign doesn't even have Larry's name on it, even though he's had this office since he retired years ago as the pastor of the Baptist church two blocks away.

It doesn't say he's there waiting for me or even hint at the odd and beautiful thing that will happen within as he listens to me and I listen to him and we both listen together in silence to the other Someone in our midst.

*Here's why I see a spiritual director.*

A few weeks ago I did a funeral, as we say in the ministry business. It was a graveside service, short and simple.

The cemetery was a mile from the Raleigh-Durham airport, and every few minutes a jet roared over our heads.

I'll always remember this funeral as the one where the casket began to roll away from me as I placed my hand on it and spoke the words "Ashes to ashes, dust to dust." The funeral director leapt to his feet and steadied it from the other end. He assured me afterward we had been in no danger, but I have my doubts. I saw the look on his face.

I had never met Betty, the deceased. She was the mother of a member of the church where my wife and I are the pastors. She died of complications associated with Alzheimer's at the age of eighty-one. Betty's son told me she'd never been a churchgoer, but she made peace with God in her own way. I wondered if the handful of people there, the ones seated under the tent and the ones standing in the wind, thought death was like getting on one of those planes and taking off to a better place—peace with God being the boarding pass.

The Scripture passage I read that morning could certainly suggest as much. "In my Father's house there are many dwelling places"—that's how it reads in the prayer book I was holding, but I said "mansions" because that's how people who have ever listened to southern gospel or read the King James Version remember it. It's easy to think about death as boarding a flight, landing at a resort, and then checking into your mansion in the sky.

But I reminded them that, whether we know it or not, from the day we cry our first breath to the day we struggle for our last, God's own love is our home. God himself is the mansion in which we live here and now. In God we live and move and have our being, as Scripture says. Whether we know it or not.

I reminded them of that, but I think I might have been reminding myself.

I don't know if Betty knew it, but I know one thing: I want to. I want to know what it's like to live in the house that is God's own presence, to live there today and tomorrow, this minute and the next. And I want to be familiar with it. I want to be able to find my way around that house of love even in the dark, negotiating my way around the corners, up the stairs, into the room where I can rest. But how? How do we learn to live in this mansion now? How do we spend our days attentive to this love that surrounds us?

xii     **Abba,** give me a word

That's why I sit on that sofa every month in the last office just past the bathroom with the retired Baptist pastor twice my age sitting across from me, the coffee table with a candle on it between us. I do it because it helps me to see and find my way through this house of love in which I live.

———————

There are plenty of books about spiritual direction. I've read some of them and recommend them. There are histories and theologies and how-to's, even though I wouldn't trust a spiritual director who learned how from a book. If you read some of those books you will hear wonderful stories and get to know fascinating characters. You will learn about the early Christian monks who left the cities after the Roman Empire had become Christian and fled to the Egyptian desert where they faced and fought temptation, because when everyone was a Christian by birth, being Christian was too easy. They went to the desert to find God, and they realized they needed each other to do it. So a younger monk would visit one of the older, experienced monks—an *abba*—and say, "Abba, give me a word." That was a request for the older man to give the younger a nugget of wisdom out of the treasury of his experience. Those nuggets began to be collected, and you can still read them today in the Sayings of the Desert Fathers.

And you'll read about others as well, about the fifth- and sixth-century saints of Ireland who transformed the pagan Celtic practice of having a soul-friend, an *anam cara*, into Christian friendships in the Spirit. And about the spiritual friendship between St. Teresa of Ávila and St. John of the Cross in the sixteenth century. St. John of the Cross gave some especially dire warnings to spiritual directors who urged strenuous effort upon people seeking their advice. You'll read about St. Ignatius of Loyola, the sixteenth-century founder of the Jesuits, who assigned to a spiritual director the role of helping someone on a silent retreat interpret Scripture with the imagination.

And this: You'll read about how in 1962 Pope John XXIII inaugurated the ecumenical age by convening the Second Vatican Council.

You may have noticed how many of the people mentioned above have two letters before their names— *St.* That's because they are Roman Catholic saints. Spiritual direction was largely the business of monks and nuns and priests and the people who came to see them. But when John XXIII called that council he opened the storehouse of Roman Catholic riches to the rest of us (except for the Anglicans, who seem to have had their own key to that storehouse for some time). In the past fifty years Protestants have begun to discover the practice of spiritual direction and have noticed ways they've already been doing it.

That's what you'll read in the history, theology, and how-to books. This is not one of those books. This book is an introduction to the practice of *receiving* spiritual direction, drawn from my experience. But that history has made this story possible. It's possible now—when it wouldn't have been fifty or forty or even thirty years ago—for a thirty-four-year-old Methodist pastor to tell the story of how his relationship with his spiritual director, a retired Baptist preacher (I hope those saints are enjoying this), helped him find the God who has been there all along.

Along the way I've learned something about receiving spiritual guidance—not only in the hour with a spiritual director but also throughout life. I've learned about what you have to let go of and what you have to embrace. That's what I want to share with you, because what you have to let go of and what you have to embrace to receive spiritual direction happen to be what you have to let go of and embrace to live well in the mansion that is God's love.

---

A few weeks ago I mentioned my spiritual director in a sermon. The next Sunday morning a man in my congregation approached me before worship. I'd guess he's in his fifties. He has a wife and a son and he works at Sears. He's active in the church. He ushers often. He helps serve Communion. He's an ordinary guy.

And this is what he said: "You mentioned last week something about having a spiritual director. Can you tell me more about that? I think that's what I need. I'm not in crisis. I don't need counseling. But I feel like God is working on me, leading me to something, and I don't know what. It feels like I'm at a crossroads, and I need someone to help me figure out which way to go next."

For every person who comes and asks, how many more are there who are beginning to sense that God is more *there* than they had ever thought, but who don't know how valuable a spiritual friendship can be to get to know, follow, and even love that God?

Maybe you are one of them.

Two weeks later another man in his late thirties asked if he could take me to lunch. He wanted to tell me how he's grown in his faith over the past few years. He's begun reading a psalm and meditating every morning because, he said, he wants to be better at staying focused on Christ throughout his day. He wondered what I thought about this. I told him he was discovering on his own a very ancient way of praying.

He didn't know what to call it, but he was looking for spiritual direction. How many more like him are out there—Methodists, Baptists, Presbyterians, seekers, and doubters—who don't know that you can seek *and* find, most often with someone's help?

I hope my experience might make this treasure of the Christian tradition available to even more people. Maybe the words Larry spoke to me, when I asked for them like those ancient monks and even when I did not, will speak to you as well and help you find your way through anger and pride, transitions and grief. And I hope what I have learned about receiving spiritual guidance—about longing and finding, releasing and offering, trusting and attending—can help you as you seek to hear a word of guidance, whether that's from a spiritual director, a friend, a spouse, or the Spirit.

Maybe what I have learned will whet your appetite to know better the God who is already there and start you asking questions, so that eventually you might find your way to an office, or a family room, or even a kitchen table where someone will be waiting, someone who has lived in God's house for so long they can help you make yourself at home there too.

---

# one

# Longing

Ayoung man just out of college and beginning a master of divinity degree at a nearby seminary sent me an e-mail saying he'd like to talk. Lonnie came into my office and sat in one of the two newly upholstered Victorian-style low chairs I had pilfered from a sitting room in the church when my wife and I had become the co-pastors six months earlier. One of my more superficial longings had always been to have an office of my own, a quiet place to read and write and think and work. When Ginger and I became co-pastors of this church, she got the real senior pastor's office—the one with two doors and two chambers, the outer chamber with the big oak desk and the couch and rocking chairs, appropriate for looking important and doing marriage counseling and having small meetings to discuss budgets and the like—and a small inner office, what I call the inner sanctum, the private reading, writing, and praying room of the senior pastor. I'm not bitter that she got the grander space. It is also the office people go to when they have a question or a complaint, because it has a gold engraved plaque on the door that says "Pastor." People know where to find her.

I got the storage room tucked away in the corner of the church's library, a quiet, out-of-the-way room with no more than a few boxes and piles of books when we arrived. We quickly found an unused desk, and I put two rickety wooden chairs next to one another so that I might show at least minimal hospitality by inviting someone to sit. And then someone told me these would not do, even for the pastor with the library closet office. He told me about the two Victorian green chairs. I moved them in and thought they would do until I had time to find something more my style. But they are still here, and they are the chairs people like Lonnie sit in, and sometimes cry in, and often laugh in when they have made a discovery and want to talk to me about it.

Lonnie seemed a little unsure how exactly to put into words what he needed to say. But it ended up something like this: I'm a new husband and a young man and a Christian, and there's a lot of stuff I don't know, especially about how to be good and faithful at any of these things. And I don't know how to pray. And I want to love God. My own dad was a pretty bad example of how to live, especially how to love. I want more than he had to show me. I want to be holy as a husband and as a Christian and eventually as a father, but I don't know how.

So far so good. Then he dropped the bomb.

"I was wondering if you might be able to mentor me."

I hope he didn't notice me glance over my shoulder to see if there was an old, wise-looking, gray-haired man standing behind me, to whom he might have been talking. But no, he was looking at me and talking to me, and he must have thought that the two gray hairs in my otherwise dark brown goatee qualified me as wise. And while at that moment I felt like an amateur—all the ancient teachers on spiritual direction would tell you to find someone with more knowledge and experience than I possessed—I did understand one thing. I understood his longing, the longing to learn a life with God, to pray, to live well, the longing for guidance from someone wise. I had discovered the same longing in myself a few years earlier.

Beneath the longing for an office of my own or a plaque on my door or a big desk that made me look important, I had discovered a longing for God and for someone who could show me how to find the God I was longing for.

The search for spiritual direction begins with a discovery. Not many people begin relationships of spiritual direction—or begin practicing *any* of the spiritual disciplines—because someone told them to or they read in a book like this one that having a spiritual guide is a good idea, even though it is. You begin the search for direction in the ways of prayer and in a life lived in the house of God's love because you have discovered a longing. I know this was the case for me, and I suspect it is the case for most others.

———————

I had an old, gray-haired man in my life for almost thirty-four years. He was even wise sometimes. I called him Dad.

Dad was fifty-five when I was born, so his hair was thinning and gray as far back as I can remember. When my brother and I were kids, one of our favorite games was to stand behind Dad as he sat in his green recliner watching the Chicago Cubs lose on a Saturday afternoon and play with his hair. We'd comb it the wrong way, make it stand up straight, then watch it slowly begin to fall. Dad rented a small sales office in a beauty parlor, so we spent more hours than we can count watching women get shampoos and perms and sit under the domed dryers with curlers in their hair. After all that, we thought we knew what we were doing. But we never dared try to curl or cut or color his silvery tufts. We would just run the black comb he always had slipped in his back pocket through his hair and feel its silkiness with our fingers.

Dad was typical of his generation—he didn't speak much about things of the heart or the soul, so I didn't learn this stuff from him. He taught us a lot, mostly by example, not by having heart-to-hearts. Men of his generation don't have heart-to-hearts. They work. They watch baseball. They throw baseballs with their kids. They teach them to fish. Dad taught me how to golf and to tie a tie. He taught me things he didn't even know he was teaching me, so now when I play with my own children, or wear tennis shoes with my khakis, or I don't care if the blue in my plaid shirt matches the blue of my sweater, I can see his influence.

He taught by example—I learned by osmosis. But there are regions of my soul this kind of teaching never touched.

One thing Dad didn't do was talk about faith or God. If he had a rich inner life, and he might have had, I had no way to know it. Not only was Dad typical of his generation in this way, Dad was also a midwesterner. Born in Indiana, he spent the summers of his youth in Chicago. He lived the rest of his life in Indiana, except for the few years he was in the Army Air Corps. And there is something about midwesterners—they don't wear their inner life on their shirtsleeves. While there is much of my dad's life I can see in myself, there is one part of his life that stayed a mystery to me—his soul.

Dad's faith was the habitual churchgoing kind. He loved going to church. He was a traveling salesman, and whenever he was gone over a weekend he would bring home the bulletin from the United Methodist Church where he had worshiped on Sunday morning. When he was home he was always the first in the car on Sunday, not just to warm the car on cold days or cool it on warm days, but because of his eagerness to get to church and shake hands with the friends he hadn't seen in a week. Many Sundays he was an usher, and he relished the job of standing at his post and greeting worshipers with a handshake, a bulletin, and a jolly smile.

I think I learned this from him as well, because I am a habitual churchgoer, always the first one ready in my house, and not just because I'm the preacher.

But I didn't learn prayer, how to understand the motions of pain and sorrow, joy and hope that are like tides in the soul's depths. His life shed no light on that for me. I had grown up in a house with a father who taught me everything other fathers teach their kids. But I didn't learn the one thing I needed most—how to live in the house of the Father, in that Love that is our truest home while we are here.

When I turned thirty, I began to discover this longing— a longing for God and for someone who could show me how to love God. I wanted a fatherlike figure who could help me peer into my own soul and not be overcome by the darkness or blinded by the light. As my own life began to settle—graduate school was ending and I had a family and a job—I began to sense an emptiness in soul-depths I never knew I had.

———

When I was eighteen, I moved out of my father's house to go to college. I'd had an experience of God (that's another story) and felt called to be a preacher. I went to college and studied religion and philosophy, and I discovered something called *theology*—the reasoned and systematic investigation of Christian belief and practice. And I was taken. From that point on I wanted to be a theologian. I thought being a theologian would make me the best pastor possible.

I somehow missed what the early Christian monk Evagrius of Pontus had to say about theologians: "If you are a theologian you truly pray. If you truly pray you are a theologian."

I skipped the so-called practical courses in seminary and stuck with the heady seminars—Karl Barth, Thomas Aquinas, Aristotle, who wasn't a theologian, obviously, but was influential on the theologians I liked best. And after three years, I finished a master of divinity degree, and four years later I was a year away from finishing my PhD. I was almost a theologian.

I had never given up on the idea of being a preacher—there was something almost romantic for me about being a pastor-theologian, a resident scholar in a church who could answer all the congregants' questions, teach with eloquence, write articles and books on the side, attend conferences, and teach a course or two at the nearest college or seminary. So my wife and I asked our bishop to appoint us to a church together, where we could share one job and have time for our children and for me to finish my degree and keep reading and writing. The bishop agreed, and in June 2005 we loaded our two boys in the station wagon, hoped the moving truck would find the way, and drove to Christ United Methodist Church, a small rural congregation six miles outside of Louisburg, North Carolina.

And here, armed with brains in my head and feet in my shoes, as Dr. Seuss put it, I began to discover the poverty of my spirit.

One of the duties I inherited as pastor was teaching two adult weekday Bible studies, one on Tuesday morning, the other on Tuesday night. A small group of seniors had been meeting every Tuesday morning for years before I got there. The evening class had been meeting together for fifteen years, and they would tell you, if you asked them, that they were the backbone of the church, the most committed and stalwart members—and they were right. They served on all the committees, did most of the work to prepare for church activities such as potlucks and the fall festival, and were probably the biggest givers to the church. These two groups were used to having the pastor every Tuesday come and talk to them about Scripture. So when Ginger and I were dividing up tasks, I got the Tuesday Bible studies.

Early in that first year we were studying the book of Ephesians. I spent Mondays preparing. I read commentaries. Sometimes I translated the text. I tried to figure it out so I could help them figure it out.

And then something disconcerting happened. I discovered verses I couldn't figure out. And it seemed as though these verses were speaking directly to me.

The book of Ephesians has some wonderful passages, but the verses I remember most, because they were the verses God used to awaken me to some deeper realities of life with God about which I had been unaware, were from chapter five. As we muddled through, we came to these verses: "Try to find out what is pleasing to the Lord" and "So do not be foolish, but understand what the will of the Lord is." In a way I had never experienced before, these verses spoke to me, not as a puzzle to be figured out, an academic exercise in discovering what some ancient writer meant, but as if they were addressed to me—*Roger, do you know what is pleasing to the Lord? Do you know what the Lord's will is? Do you know how to discern?*

I didn't know how to discern. I didn't know how to listen. I didn't know what it meant to find out what is pleasing to the Lord. This was a mystery to me. And it was a mystery to the folks in the Bible study. I was the deaf leading the deaf.

This experience set off a chain reaction. I began to notice other verses in the Bible: "pray without ceasing, give thanks in all circumstances"; "discern what is the will of the Lord"; "present your bodies as a living sacrifice, holy and acceptable to God"; "be perfect as your heavenly Father is perfect." These weren't verses any longer about God—they were words to me about the mystery of life with God, and they highlighted one thing—my poverty.

But they were also the beginning of a longing for someone who could show me the way.

When I wasn't at the church, I was either visiting or at home with my two young boys. And my growing longing made me ask: What are they learning from me? What can they learn from me? What do I have to teach them? With a pair of blue eyes and a pair of brown eyes looking at me, these boys were not old enough to tell me what they needed or expected, but they were already old enough to start imitating—old enough to learn. What were they learning from me? As we lived in this church-owned house together, what did I have that I could teach them about living in the house that is the love of the Father for the Son in the Spirit?

How could I teach them if no one had taught me?

———

I'm just guessing, but you have very likely already begun to make this discovery. You are becoming aware of at least a vague sense of longing for God—maybe not yet the deer-panting-for-streams-of-flowing-water kind of longing for

God. It may be a simple restlessness. But it's there and you know it.

And I suspect this longing for God is already associated with a longing for guidance—why else would you read books on the spiritual life?

Where can you go for help? Who can show you the way?

This is where the search for spiritual direction begins. But it might be some time before you come to the conclusion that what you need is a flesh-and-blood spiritual director, or before you find the right one. In the meantime, there are ways you can deepen this discovery and continue to cultivate the longing. These are practices that can take us all the way through the practice of spiritual direction, but they are particularly appropriate here at the beginning, at the recognition of that initial sense of desire—for God and for guidance.

And they are quite simple. The first is—find a pen and a few blank pages and begin to write about it. Don't know what to write? Try writing what I call a "longing list." At the top of a blank sheet of paper write, "What do I want?" And then begin to make a list of the things you are longing for. Don't try to be pious. No one is looking over your shoulder to see if you are longing for the right things. Just begin. You might want to commit to writing for five minutes without stopping or thinking too much. Just write.

If I were writing my longing list today, it would probably begin with "a new van." It would have the names of a few books. Now that we have two boys and a baby girl, the list would say, somewhere, "a little peace and quiet." Sleep would be on it for sure (which is more of a spiritual longing than most would think). Maybe the van would come up again—or at least a new door on the old van. The list would be boring, mundane.

If yours is boring and mundane, that's okay. Maybe you'll need to start again tomorrow. Do this for three days. What do I want? What am I longing for? Write.

Sooner or later, I imagine, depending on how far along you are in making the discovery, the words on the list are going to be more like this: peace, rest (not in the "I-need to-take-a-nap" sense, but in the "rest-for-my-weary-soul" sense), quiet, hope, love—or *to be* loved—life, strength. Maybe you write a line from a hymn you used to sing growing up—strength for today and bright hope for tomorrow.

And then maybe the word "God" will show up on the list, or maybe just "Love," but this time you wrote it with a capital letter. Perhaps, "Direction." You long to know where you're headed and how to get there.

It's useless to ask which of these longings are better—a new van is real and relevant to me right now. The point is not to judge the things closer to the top of the list. But the pen can be like an archaeologist's pick, helping us slowly move through the layers of longing that characterize all of our lives, to get below the everyday, obvious longings and to get to the bottom, to the foundational longings that in some mysterious ways give shape to all the rest.

The other practice is spiritual reading. Reading the stories of others, in whom a longing for God has been awakened and who have pursued that longing, is a way not only of refining our own longing but also of cultivating it as well, of deepening it.

But let me warn you, spiritual reading has a danger, and we should be aware of that danger from the outset.

Let me say it as pointedly as possible: Reading about prayer, or the memoirs of saints and monks, has a subtle way of preventing prayer by replacing it. It can inhibit a life of prayer and obstruct our journey toward God if we let ourselves think that this kind of reading *is* prayer, that it *is* the journey itself. You read instead of pray.

Prayer is mysterious. The silence it calls for can be off-putting. It's easier to pick up a book and let ourselves be moved by the story of someone else's life. If this happens, spiritual reading can distract us from our own longing for God as that longing gets diverted into a search for deeper and deeper spiritual *insight*—a new way of praying, or a new understanding of God. We begin to peruse the shelves of the bookstore looking for the newest and latest in spirituality (maybe that's how you came across this book) when we would be better served by getting our butts in our chairs and reading the Psalms.

I only know this from my own experience. I reached the point where I had to establish a firm rule for myself: You, Roger, are not allowed to read about prayer until you have spent time praying. To choose to read instead of pray is to succumb to sloth—laziness in the life of prayer. I have some expertise in succumbing to this particular temptation.

But once we recognize the danger and establish whatever boundaries we need to avoid it, spiritual reading can help us recognize and cultivate the growing sense of longing for God and the sense of our own aimlessness, thus deepening our sense of need for direction. When we read about the prayer lives of others, it's like looking at a beautiful vision of what is possible—we might not know *how* it is possible, but we see it and want it. It allows us to ask: could God do this in my life? When we read how others have learned to live in the house that is God's love, we can become increasingly inspired to live in that house ourselves. If we already have the longing, this kind of reading can help us deepen it and spur us along the journey as we search for someone who can show us the way. The desire for direction begins to grow as we recognize the gap that exists between the shape of the lives we are reading about—the graceful ways their lives inhabit the house of God's love—and the fumbling ways we trip over the doorjamb just trying to enter.

As we read we might begin to have a growing sense that a book, as useful as it is to awaken in us a desire for God and show us our need for direction, cannot replace the person who sits across the coffee table and listens to our lives. Books aren't so good at listening.

This is what happened to me. I began to read books about prayer and spiritual memoirs. I devoured them, especially the ones that pointed to a contemplative way of living and praying. They showed me what was possible. They were the stories of real lives that were so close to God they might as well have been one with God. Maybe they were. They talked about resting in God. And I saw in them a mirror of my own longing for rest. But I also asked the questions: how is this kind of prayerful life possible, and who can show me the way?

Where will I find a spiritual guide?

———

I stood to preach between two oak lecterns, the one to my right the pulpit, the one to my left a little smaller, where people stood to read Scripture and sing solos and make announcements. With nothing between me and the people, I could see each one of them well. Like Santa Claus, I knew who was naughty and who was nice—or at least who was sleeping and who was awake. Bill and Jan sat to my right, four rows back from the front, right behind Bob and Diana. Behind Bill and Jan sat Jack and Ruth. Jack was Bill's cousin, who began coming more regularly after we arrived and was always asleep by the time the sermon started. Ethel sat on the back row on the left side, where she kept a pillow on the pew to mark her spot and make the pew easier on her back. I knew them all—their names, their stories.

Closer to the front were two busy boys, two of the three kids in the sanctuary, sitting with whichever patient parishioner had volunteered to sit with them that day, two boys who loved to come to church, who walked with me across the field with smiles every Sunday morning. The field that on other days was our playground for chasing balls or each other on Sunday was a passage, and we crossed it with joy.

Standing between those lecterns in front of these people, I preached.

Sunday after Sunday I had a growing sense that I was preaching out of my own poverty, not a poverty of knowledge, but a poverty of prayer. I spoke about that which I did not know. Maybe my woven flax alb hid from them my poverty, and maybe it hid it from me for a while, and maybe I hid it behind book learning and funny stories, my two defenses against this one fact: they looked to me as a spiritual leader, and I needed to be led.

The stained glass window behind me was a picture of where I wanted to go. Above the altar, built into the wall and backlit by a light outside, was a colorful window, the same one in almost every small church—Jesus praying, perhaps in the Garden of Gethsemane, although he looked too serene for that. Kneeling, elbows on a tree stump, light shining on him from the clouds, blue and red robes, no doubt more expensive than the ones he really would have worn. And here was the most stunning part. Just below Jesus was a name: Alex Wilson. Likely the man who gave the money for the window, I saw his name there as a symbol. Here is a picture of the Trinity— the conversation of the Son with the Father in the Spirit, and Alex Wilson was being drawn into that. How did he get there, so close to that conversation? It was as if that window were Wilson's new home, the home all of us are looking for—a home in God's own life.

I wanted to be there. I wasn't sure how, but I wanted to be drawn into that divine conversation. I wanted the kind of prayer that pastor and theologian Jason Byassee writes about when he says, "Prayer is ultimately an inner-Trinitarian conversation into which we creatures are invited." I felt that I was being invited, by a discovery of my longing and my poverty, into that life, which is the conversation of love among the Father, the Son, and the Spirit.

Isn't this the point of Jesus' farewell discourse in the Gospel of John? Isn't this window—in which Alex Wilson was lucky enough to find a home—what Jesus is saying God wants for each of us? What else could he mean when he tells us to abide in his love as he abides in the Father's love? He is calling us into the home, the house that is the Son's love of the Father in the Spirit.

And this is the mystery I could explain as a theologian but felt incompetent to lead people toward because I didn't know how to abide there myself. These people who could have taught me a million things I didn't know—how to fix a lawnmower, how to clean a chicken, how to make Brunswick stew—showed up week after week looking to me to teach them the one thing I couldn't teach. Hoping I might tell them how to get their name in that window. But I had to learn myself, first.

I was Lonnie. No longer a student but a young dad and pastor and husband with more people than I needed looking to me. And I needed a guide, gray hair optional.

Here's the difference: Lonnie had a door to knock on—mine. Whose door did I have to knock on?

Whose door, I wonder, do you have to knock on?

# two

# Finding

Every day a small blue car with a driver and three passengers and an orange sign on top that read "Student Driver" reminded me of what I was longing for. Bill, the man in the front passenger seat, was the finance committee chairman of our church. He had been the finance chair as long as anyone could remember, and his brother Al had been the trustees chair longer than that, even though every January, at the first trustees' meeting of the year, he announced that he wanted to step down if someone else would volunteer to be the chair. The few moments of silence said that no one else wanted the job—who would want to be the person we called in the middle of the night when there was a leak at the parsonage, or on a Sunday afternoon when the dishwasher was broken? But I suspect that silence also spoke what we all knew: Al loved the job, and his announcement of his readiness to step down was more pro forma than it was heartfelt. These two brothers, Bill and Al, were the backbone and the memory and the worker bees of the church.

After his early retirement from teaching high school science, Bill taught driver education, more to give himself something to do while his wife curled, cut, and dyed hair in her downtown beauty parlor five days a week. He hated the classroom part of the course—to get out of that was the reason he retired early. But he loved the driving, because he loved this county where he grew up. I imagine nothing gave him more pleasure than to drive these county roads with these teenagers, telling them whose farm this had been, and who had lived there, and how things used to be before the children started leaving the farms for the cities and everything changed.

Every day he drove with his students past the church. They would use the circle drive behind the church to turn around, or they stopped at the church for a restroom break. Most afternoons I would be outside playing with the boys in the field of grass between the parsonage and the church, and we would stop and wave at Bill. He would flash us his characteristic smile—the smile I always wanted to see when I was preaching because it told me I was getting close to something, perhaps something true—and he'd flip his right hand up in a gentle wave as they drove past. It made my boys feel special. They didn't know that as the most recognizable man in Louisburg, cruising the town and the county every day in that blue car, Bill smiled and waved at hundreds of people. They just knew it was Bill who went to our church, and he was waving at us.

Bill could risk a wave and a glance. But the driver couldn't. White knuckles grasping the wheel, these drivers were neophytes. They were still learning the signs and the roads and the ways of country driving. But they were lucky to have a Bill next to them as they learned. They didn't have to go it alone.

Life with God is not so clear-cut as learning to drive a car. Making a home in the house that is God's love and living in that home day by day has its mysteries, its moments of confusion. The signs aren't as clear and unambiguous as the signs along the roadside. There are books to help you understand living in this house, and those can help. But sooner or later you have to leave the classroom and the books behind and get out on the road. Then it can seem like you are absolutely alone, and the only thing to do is grab the wheel with your own white knuckles and find your own way, doing the best you can.

Unless you have a Bill. Unless there is someone next to you who has driven these roads before. Who can remind you to relax. Who can help you find your way.

There was no way I could have known that Bill would be the one to introduce me to the man who would become for me that more-experienced traveling companion and guide.

———————

The first time we went to the Cola Café we'd been in town just a few days, and we were exploring the downtown. Judy owned the Cola Café, a 1950s retro-style diner, decorated in red and white with vintage Coca-Cola pictures on the wall, and she showed us genuine southern hospitality. When she found out we were new in town she made a milkshake for each boy and gave them to us for free.

This time it was a rainy Friday night, and we were not going to have milkshakes. We would be eating Judy's famous spaghetti casserole because that's what Jan had ordered for Bill's sixty-fifth birthday, which Judy was catering.

We ran from the car in the rain and ducked quickly into the diner, and it felt as if we were at a church potluck. All the people there were the same people we saw every week at church. They were Bill's relatives and friends, the people he had worked with and played with, and in a way that could only happen in a small country church, they were the same people he worshiped with. In this small diner were the people we visited in the hospital, taught in Sunday school, and preached to on Sunday mornings.

Except for one couple.

I noticed a man standing to the back of the diner who looked familiar. In fact, I had a funny feeling that I knew his name was Larry. But I had no idea how I knew him. He wasn't a church member. And he had never visited our church. And I'd met the close relatives of most of the people in the room, so if he was related he must have been a distant cousin from out of town, which wouldn't explain how I recognized him. So I began to ask around.

"Carol," I said to our volunteer pianist, "do you know that guy standing next to the ice-cream counter? I think his name is Larry, but I have no idea how I would know that." Carol didn't know him, and the next three people I asked didn't either. An extrovert would have walked right up to him, extended a hand, and introduced himself. But I'm no extrovert. So I spent the dinner wondering how I knew this guy.

Ginger and I sat with George and Barbara at dinner. George was Bill's cousin and the chair of our church's administrative board. Ginger had to do all the talking, because my mind was completely occupied. I was so busy trying to figure out how I knew this man and that his name was Larry, I didn't even notice whether the spaghetti casserole was as wonderful as everyone said it would be.

When the meal was finished, Bill walked over to our table.

"There's someone I want you to meet. Have you met Larry Williams yet?"

His name *is* Larry, I thought.

"Larry is retired from being the pastor at Louisburg Baptist Church." Louisburg Baptist was the downtown Baptist church, just two blocks from the Cola Café. "I taught high school with his wife for seventeen years; that's how I know him. They are a really neat couple, and I think you would enjoy knowing them." So we got out of our seats and followed Bill toward where Larry and his wife were sitting.

When Bill introduced us, I said to Larry, "You look familiar. I even knew your name was Larry, but I have no idea how I would know you. I've been a student at Duke Divinity School since nineteen-ninety-eight. Have you ever done anything there?"

"In ninety-eight and ninety-nine I was a spiritual formation group leader at the divinity school."

Mystery solved. Spiritual formation groups were mandatory small groups in which all incoming divinity school students had to participate. They were a new attempt to remedy the fact that students at divinity school learned a lot about God, but it didn't help much in relating to God or in teaching other people how. My group wasn't effective at doing what it was intended to do. Larry hadn't been my group leader, but at student orientation all the group leaders were introduced to the incoming class. I would have seen him there and probably in the hallways.

We stood and chatted for a while, and I had the sense that there was something special about Larry. We talked about the theologians we liked to read, and somewhere in the conversation he mentioned reading the *Christian Century*, a Christian magazine for mainline Protestants, and I thought at that moment that our two subscriptions must be the only two in Franklin County.

We had been in Franklin County for about ten months, and the isolation we felt was overwhelming. We were having a difficult time adjusting to rural life, and as transplanted city-dwellers we were clearly out of place. We already loved the people of our church, but we longed to be in relationships with some people with whom we didn't have to be "on," as we did even at a birthday party on a Friday night. And as we talked to Larry and Zelma, they not only seemed like people we would love to be friends with, they also seemed to be the kind of wise elders we could learn from. After college and graduate school, Larry had been pastor of a Baptist church in western North Carolina, campus minister at a woman's college in Raleigh, and then pastor here in Louisburg for twenty years.

"Late in my pastoral career I began to wonder how as a pastor I could be a better spiritual guide to my church," said Larry as we continued our conversation. "I started reading widely on prayer and spiritual direction. Several years ago I received training in spiritual direction. Ever since I've been leading spiritual formation groups at Duke Divinity, I lead a retreat for pastors called 'The Pastor as Spiritual Guide,' and I give spiritual direction. It's funny how in my retirement God has reshaped my vocation and given me new, good work to do."

Have you ever had the experience that divine providence was a little more at work in your life than usual? I never could have imagined—no one could have, because the chances were so slim—that on a Friday night in this town of 3,000, I would meet this man with such similar interests to mine, who had asked the same questions I was asking now, had worked through them throughout his life, and was now ready to help others find their way.

We said goodbye to Bill and Jan, wished him a happy birthday again, thanked Judy for the spaghetti that everyone had told me was excellent, and headed home to relieve the babysitter.

On the way home, our silence only broken by the pattering of rain on the car roof and the regular swish of the windshield wipers, I finally said out loud to Ginger what I had been thinking. "I don't know if I want them to be our friends, or if I want him to be my spiritual director."

A few more moments of silence, then Ginger said, "I think you do know."

If I had already had a spiritual director, this is exactly the kind of thing I would talk with him or her about—is this an opportunity God is opening for me? Should I call him and start spiritual direction? Is this the right thing for me? But I didn't, so I went to my default setting: read. Thus began my crash course in spiritual direction.

I began reading to learn more about what this kind of spiritual relationship involved, what it would be like, and what would be required of me. I'd already read enough to know that something like spiritual direction was what I was looking for. As Thomas Merton said, "Spiritual direction is a moral necessity for anyone who is trying to deepen his life of prayer."

What I discovered surprised me—there is no one way to do spiritual direction, and it takes many shapes.

In the Christian tradition it has long been acknowledged (from the days that Jesus himself said "Follow me" and from the time he told his disciples to go and make disciples, teaching, and baptizing, and helping people obey) that the Christian life—that life lived with God through Christ in the Spirit—is a life of apprenticeship. As Jonathan Wilson-Hartgrove has written, "Like woodworking or plumbing, the craft of life with God is learned by practicing it in apprenticeship to others who know the way better than ourselves." And when this apprenticeship has gone under the name of spiritual direction, the shape of the practice has been varied.

I discovered this practice first in my readings of the Desert Fathers and Mothers. These Christians fled to the deserts of Egypt and Palestine to escape the corruption of city life and the compromised Christian living they thought that city life necessarily entailed. They left for lives of solitude and silence, to do battle with the demons, to work out their salvation with fear and trembling. Most lived in loosely organized communities as hermits, each in his own hut, called a cell, but also sharing a common life. These communities were often organized around an abba or amma, a parent-like monk who had become known for his or her way of living with God. The other monks would come to this older monk and say, "Give me a word," asking for a word of advice on how to progress in this life they had chosen. Sometimes the question was very specific—for instance, "Why are these particular thoughts troubling me?"—and sometimes it was simply an invitation to offer a word of wisdom, as when a brother went to Abba Moses and asked him for advice, and Moses replied, "Go and sit in your cell, and your cell will teach you everything."

Spiritual direction in this form lives up to the name *direction*, for the older, experienced monk embodied the wisdom of the tradition of the desert, and the younger monk learned that tradition by obedience—by taking the direction of the elder.

For these monks living a life of battling demons and temptation, obeying a spiritual father was a life-or-death matter. "Nothing harms the monk so much," said Abba Theonas, "and gives such happiness to the demons, as when he conceals his thoughts from his spiritual father." Who could survive this life of austerity and prayer without the wisdom of these abbas and ammas?

But not all spiritual direction has looked so one-way. Even the different names applied to the practice indicate a variety, for some prefer to talk about spiritual friendship and others spiritual guidance. These different ways of naming the practice acknowledge the same reality that a life of prayer lived in God's house of love is necessarily learned in the company of others, but they indicate greater mutuality. As Christianity took root in Ireland, the Celtic practice of having an *anam cara*, a "soul-friend" or spiritual advisor, influenced the Christian practice of spiritual direction there. There soul-friends could be men or women, laypeople or priests, but, as the name implies, the stress in this tradition was on the mutuality of the relationship. A Celtic proverb speaks of the importance of this relationship: "Anyone without a soul-friend is a body without a head."

There are also short-term forms of spiritual direction and long-term relationships of spiritual direction. Someone might see a spiritual director for a short time to get aid in discernment around a particular issue— vocation, for instance. You might see a spiritual director once a month for four months. Or a Quaker might call a clearness committee, inviting a group of three or four trusted friends to ask you honest, open questions for two or three hours to help you discern around a particular issue. Or you simply might call a spiritual friend on the phone and say, "Hey, I've got a problem, a quandary, and I'm wondering if you can listen for a while to help me figure out where God is leading."

I knew something more long-term was what I was longing for. I knew my apprenticeship in the Spirit would take more than a few months. You can't learn to be a plumber in a few short months, and I doubted you could learn to live in the house of God's love, and be attentive to living in that house throughout your days, in a few sessions. I needed someone who would stick by me as I learned and grew.

As the practice of spiritual direction developed, the practice of going to an abba or amma or having a soul-friend grew into a more formal discipline, the practice of which required training. As the practice became formalized, an individual had to learn how to be a spiritual director—aside from possessing the gift or being recognized in the community as someone who could help to discern God's Spirit at work. St. Ignatius of Loyola, for example, in the development of his *Spiritual Exercises* not only presented a clear picture of the role of spiritual director, but, in the words of Kenneth Leech, he also laid the "foundation for the development of a whole school of spiritual direction." A person comes to an Ignatian spiritual director, who gives the exercises and then meets with the directee to help him or her in discerning the way God is leading. The director must be trained and experienced in this particular method.

In my cursory reading in spiritual direction I was able to learn things that helped me to have a sense of what I might be getting myself into. On the one hand, I learned that spiritual direction can be a casual, spiritual friendship, one involving no formal training, and perhaps no formal acknowledgment that spiritual direction is what is going on. But it can also be more intentional, as with the desert monks and the Celts, where it was clear who the abba or who the soul-friend was. On the other hand, spiritual direction can be very defined—a specific method, as in the Ignatian style, with a director trained to lead the directee through very defined exercises, the aim of which is to help the directee discern the particular movement of God in his or her life.

If you are still in this early stage, having recognized your own longing for an abba or amma to whom you can apprentice yourself in a life of prayer, in life with God, but have not found one yet, it would be a good idea to spend some time thinking about what you are seeking in a spiritual guide: Someone who can give you very specific advice, who will take a firm, directive approach? Someone who will take long walks with you, listening and reflecting, and helping you see God's movement in your life? Someone who can journey with you over a short period of time as you discern God's presence and movement in your life around a particular issue, or someone who can walk beside you as you seek to make a home in God's love your whole life long? Thinking about these questions might help to refine your search as you begin.

But remember, you shouldn't be too rigid ahead of time. It's impossible to say in advance how God's Spirit will move and how God can form a lasting and beneficial spiritual relationship out of unlikely friends.

And then the search begins. Here my individual experience won't be much help, because I doubt getting invited to a birthday party at the Cola Café will help you find a spiritual director. There's nothing scientific about the search for a spiritual director. Simply begin asking around. Talk to a pastor you know, or a priest. If they don't know of a spiritual director, they might know someone in spiritual direction. Along with a list of counselors and therapists to whom I can refer people, I have a list of spiritual directors in the area. The best way is to start talking and asking. Sooner or later, someone will know what you're talking about. Someone will have a name to give you. After a while, you might have three or four names. At that point, it's time to call and make some appointments. Then see how the Spirit leads.

After my own crash course in the history and practice of spiritual direction, I knew a few things about the practice. But I didn't know how Larry approached it, or what it would be like with him. But I did know it was time to make an appointment.

When I walked into Larry's office—his cell—I did what I always do. I inspected my surroundings. He stood from behind his desk and greeted me, and I let my eyes dart around the room, taking it in. He obviously didn't spend his days in his office like a desert monk in his cell, weaving baskets. I could tell Larry was a reader. Opposite the door was a wall of bookshelves that rose halfway up the wall. Commentaries. Theology. Books on prayer and spirituality—no surprise. I also wasn't surprised to see many of the same books I had on my bookshelves. Framed on the wall, above the bookshelves, were photos of the churches where he had been a pastor. I recognized one as the Baptist church two blocks away. File cabinets ranged along the adjacent wall, with a CD player on top and a stack of CDs. Taped to the side was a framed picture that looked like a grandchild had made it, which said "Keep in Touch." Some Boston Red Sox paraphernalia. To the left of the door sat a couch against the wall. In front of the couch was a coffee table with a lit votive candle and some magazines stacked so that the publication date of each was just visible. One stack was the *Christian Century*, the other a devotional magazine called *Alive Now*. Across from the coffee table was a straight-backed sitting chair with a floor lamp next to it. I assumed that's where Larry would sit.

One piece of art caught my attention, and it still does. I've searched everywhere for a reprint but haven't been able to find one. The poster is a black-and-white photograph of a father tossing his toddler into the air, who has a smile of excitement and delight I'm very familiar with, since I've seen it so many times on my own children's faces. At the bottom right corner of the picture is a quote attributed to St. Francis de Sales: "Nothing is so strong as gentleness, nothing is so gentle as real strength."

I didn't know it then, but now I can see how that poster encapsulates Larry's method of spiritual direction— gentle strength and strong gentleness. His way is always accepting and never judgmental. In that way, he's truly gentle. But he's also willing to challenge me, to encourage me to name the ways I'm deciding *not* to listen to God, and to ask myself why. I have heard him say in another context that challenging is one of the most difficult things a spiritual director does, but he has been able to do it out of his gentleness and my life is better off for it. His way of directing has shown it to be true—nothing is so strong as true gentleness.

But I didn't know all that then. All I knew were the few things he told me about spiritual direction and how he went about it.

And the first thing he said was the most important: In spiritual direction, the Holy Spirit is the real director. All we are doing is looking together at my life—my desires, fears, doubt, perplexities—so that I can become more attentive and available to the Holy Spirit's direction in my life.

At the time, the idea of listening and responding to God's ongoing presence in my life seemed too good to be true. I certainly liked the idea of the Holy Spirit being my spiritual director, but I was also glad that I got to learn how to let the Spirit lead in the company of a human being I could see and hear.

He also told me that spiritual direction is different from therapy, even though we might deal with the same issues, because in spiritual direction no part of our lives is off limits. The difference is in the way in which we view our lives. When we go to a therapist we usually have a "presenting issue"—a problem to be solved. Anxiety. Depression. Relationship trouble. And then we work with the therapist to help solve or at least lessen the effects of the presenting problem.

"But in spiritual direction," Larry said, "we view life under the God lens. We look at life from the perspective of our desire for God, and with the presumption that God's grace is always at work, even in our problems."

That means that sometimes we talk about problems, struggles, and issues, but not necessarily to solve them. We look at them for signs of God's grace in the midst of them, and as pointers to our deepest desire and longings. Fortunately, discovering God at work in the midst of our problems goes a long way toward alleviating them.

The Westminster Shorter Catechism begins by asking, "What is the chief end of man?" The answer: "Man's chief end is to glorify God and to enjoy him forever." In spiritual direction we look at life as tending toward God's glory. We look at our lives as good creations divinely redeemed, and as the playground for the Spirit's transforming work. Sometimes that means thinking about deep problems.

But sometimes for me it means thinking about playing with my children, or my daily walk from parsonage to church, or when and how I pray. It means learning how to give thanks in all things. And if a problem gets solved along the way, to give thanks for that as well.

After these introductory explanations of what spiritual direction is about, Larry got down to the nuts and bolts: You show up. We sit. I light the candle to remind us of Christ's presence in our midst. I take off my shoes, because I believe this work during this time is holy ground, and you are welcome to take off your shoes as well. Then we spend some time in silence. I'll ask one of us to say a prayer after the silence. And then you begin. You talk about whatever you want. This is your time. This is your life.

After five years, I haven't yet taken off my shoes.

———————

A few weeks later I was back. This time there were no preliminaries. The candle was already lit. Larry greeted me warmly at his office door and invited me to sit. There was some brief chit-chat, as there almost always is now.

The child in the poster, suspended in the air with the look of joy on his face, seemed to be looking down at me, as if to say, "It's time to let go, to trust, and even have fun."

"I'll have the prayer after our silence," Larry said, as he began to untie his shoes and take them off like a real, live Mr. Rogers right in front of me. As he took off his shoes, he reminded me that during the silence I might want to sit comfortably with my feet on the floor and my hands resting in my lap. I shifted in my seat as he placed his shoes next to him, then we closed our eyes and settled into the silence.

There I was, the young monk in the abba's cell, thinking I'd come for a word. Give me a word—that's what I wanted to say. I knew he had much to teach me and I had much to learn. But that's not how it would go. I would have the first word. My life was the word we would look at together. When the silence was over and he said a prayer, it would be my turn to give a word, and in that word we would listen together for a word from God.

# three

# Releasing

I was in the deli section of the grocery store to get a free sugar cookie in the plastic box under the sign that read "For Kids of All Ages: One Per Person." This plastic box is the reason my boys will come with me to the grocery store any time I want them to—this box and the free balloons when we leave.

Nibbling on my cookie, I saw someone I recognized. She was a well-known professor of religion. What she was doing in the deli section was more than sampling the provolone cheese. She did do that first, though. She reached in the sample container, stuck in a toothpick, and tasted a piece of cheese. She must have liked it. I know this not because I saw her go to the deli counter and order some cheese slices. I know this because, after she tasted the cheese, she grabbed one of the waxy pieces of paper they have so you can get a piece of cheese without touching other pieces with your hand (the same kind I used to get the cookie out of the box). Then she glanced over her left shoulder, glanced over her right shoulder, reached into the sample box, and with that piece of paper grabbed as much cheese as she could fit in her hand, shoved it into her purse, and walked away.

And after my shock subsided, but before I had a chance to judge her, I thought: that's me, and it's all of us—fist-clenched grabbers.

Have you ever tried to put a rattle into the hand of a newborn? It's almost impossible. You have to peel back each little finger, one at a time. When I've done it I've marveled at the strength of those little fingers. Harder still is getting the rattle out of the baby's fist once it's there. When the baby is older and can reach, you'd better get a strap to hold your glasses on your head. When those quick hands with their tight clasp pull your glasses off your face, good luck at getting them back.

We come into the world with our fists clenched. Maybe this is partly what the Christian tradition means when it says we were born in original sin—we start out as grabbers, like Adam and Eve. Everything around them was a gift. They had no need to grab. Yet the one thing they were not allowed to have they grabbed like glasses off God's face so they could be like God.

That's you and I, as well.

If we're lucky, somewhere along the way we meet someone or read something or lose something that makes us realize that grabbing and grasping is not the way God intended us to live. Then we spend the rest of our lives—if we're lucky—learning how to relax our grip and release. Learning how to let go, to abandon ourselves into God's care instead of grasping at every chance to be the god of our own lives. We can only hope that something along the way will help us to see that living life in and with God can only be done open-handed.

We can't live in our truest home, in the life of love that is a gift of God, by grasping and grabbing, but only by learning what poet Denise Levertov writes in her poem "The Avowal," that "no effort earns that all-surrounding grace."

Learning to let go and release, that is the first and hardest lesson I am learning in spiritual direction. What am I holding onto that God is inviting me to let go of if I want to live freely and abundantly in the house of God's love? What memory of the past do I need to release? What lust for power? What hoped-for future? What dream of fame and fortune? What anxiety? What fear? Whenever I let go, there's always something else to grab. I don't know if I'll ever learn to relax my fingers completely. I am beginning to learn how, though, one finger at a time.

But learning to release our grasp is not simply something we learn *in* spiritual direction. It's also one of the gestures of the soul that allows us to *receive* spiritual direction.

---

If you've decided to enter into spiritual direction, this lesson in letting go has already begun. You are letting go of our culture's story of the self that says we are fundamentally self-determinative individuals. We have the right to "life, liberty, and the pursuit of happiness," and we should grasp those rights and teach them to our children, and elect politicians who will protect them, and clear away every obstacle that might stand in our way, even if that obstacle is God. Perhaps that's why the founders of this country, who told us we have the rights, believed in a deity who simply got things started but stayed out of the way from then on. That's the kind of God we grabbers can get along with.

When you enter into spiritual direction you are saying, in essence, I'm going to let someone else in. I'm going to loosen my grip on self-determination because I desire to live a *God*-determined life. You might not even know what it means to live a God-determined life when you start. I certainly didn't and often think I still don't. But you can name the desire nonetheless. You've seen yourself reaching in and grabbing all the cheese, and you don't like what you saw. You are tired of grasping at the reins, of being the god of your own life.

To let God be God we release the grip on our own lives. We let go of that prized-above-all-else right to live our lives as we want, in order to let our lives find their way into God's and be lived something more like the way God wants.

"Those who want to save their life will lose it, and those who lose their life for my sake, and for the sake of the gospel, will save it," said the best Teacher ever of the art of letting go.

Just when all of this talk about letting go begins to sound quite abstract, you knock on a door. And you sit down in a room with icons and candles and crosses, or simple, bare walls. With a rug and a table and a candle, perhaps. A kneeling bench, maybe, with a book on it with lots of ribbons. And a man or a woman, probably older than you. And you sit down. And you begin to tell your stories. You let them go. You release them.

There's no way to know for sure what will happen next.

Open your mouth, and the lesson in letting go has begun.

———

The idea of letting go, especially of material things—the idea of self-denial—has long appealed to me. I don't know when it started, perhaps when I read G. K. Chesterton's little biography of St. Francis. I like to sing like Francis did, and I like to watch birds, and I saw how his poverty made him available to God and to others. I wanted to be like him. I wanted to give everything away.

I would mention this to Larry on occasion. It became one of the recurring themes of our conversations. "Jesus said 'deny yourself.' I want to do that, Larry. How can I do it? How can I do it *more*?"

I love the story of the Desert Father who, on returning from a journey, saw a thief robbing his little hut. Pretending to be a passerby who was unaware that a theft was in progress, the monk helped the thief load his possessions on a donkey and blessed him as he rode away.

"How can I be like *that*? This monk has learned to deny himself, to release everything, hasn't he, Larry? How can I learn to do that?"

My wife wasn't so enthusiastic about this growing desire to give things away, and now, looking back, I can understand why. We had recently left the city of Durham, where we lived in walking distance from Duke University and the city's best Indian restaurant. She had a full-time job as an associate pastor, and I was a graduate student on a stipend. We had friends and neighbors. We had libraries and bookstores in walking distance. We had theaters. We had Anotherthyme, the restaurant where we ate the night we got engaged, and where, when it's in season, the Aegean Sea pasta is incredible. We had a lot.

And then we decided we wanted to be pastors of a church together. That meant, as United Methodists, going wherever the bishop sent us. When we stood in front of the bishop in a line with the other ordinands and promised to itinerate—to move when the bishop thought it was a good idea and to where the bishop thought our gifts for ministry matched the needs of a local congregation—surely agreeing to such an arrangement constituted sufficient self-denial, right? Did we need to give up more?

And so we packed and moved from a house we owned to a parsonage in the country. From a city of 230,000 to six miles outside of a town of 3,000. From a house in a neighborhood with three parks to a parsonage on a lonely corner in the country where our closest neighbors were the ones buried in the church's graveyard.

And into a parsonage that was already furnished. We moved into a house with a living room couch too large for the space (so the corner section of the couch was put in the master bedroom) donated by a family for whom this couch wasn't good enough anymore. And we started sharing one job that paid the very least a church in our conference is allowed to pay a full-time pastor.

"Aren't we doing a pretty good job with the self-denial stuff?" I could hear Ginger saying to herself every time I started talking about that monk, the donkey, and the thief.

---

In spiritual direction you learn to name your desires, noticing them and asking where they come from and what they are for. This naming and noticing is done in the conviction that our deepest desires are for God. By the time you are in spiritual direction you have probably named and noticed that desire for God. But we listen to the other desires as well, assuming that they come from this most fundamental human desire for God but that once they have risen to the surface, once they have bubbled up to the place where they can be noticed or named, the desires have been shaped and molded, sometimes misshaped and twisted. Too often an ostensibly holy desire—the desire to become a self-sacrificing saint, for instance—becomes twisted to play a self-serving purpose.

"You like the idea of being a St. Francis?" Larry asked on at least one occasion after I released this story of desire.

Sometimes it's just a question—the way Larry listens to what I'm saying and reflects the words back to me in a question, as if he's holding a mirror to my soul. He's not telling me what's going on in there, or what I should think about what's going on in there, or what God might be up to in there, but simply letting me hear my own story, often in my own words, sometimes in the shape of a question, so that I can see it for what it is.

And one of the things his listening and reflecting has helped me to see is that this longing for self-denial, the idea of being the jolly, holy, and austere St. Francis, can easily be co-opted by another, less holy desire: the desire to be a somebody, a famous somebody.

It has never taken much for me to leave reality and fly into an imagined and unreal future in which I am Important (with a capital "I"), into what Archbishop of Canterbury Rowan Williams calls "self-dramatizing and fantasy."

If you'd asked me when I was in junior high school what I wanted to be when I grew up, I would have said, "I think

I'll be a concert pianist." I could close my eyes and see it: Carnegie Hall, the stage, the lights, a nine-foot Steinway, my shoulders hunched over the keys, my fingers hammering out a Rachmaninoff something-or-other (I didn't know enough to know what it would be, but it certainly would be more difficult than the arrangement of "When the Saints Go Marching In" I was supposed to be practicing at the time). When the piece was over, I imagined a moment of awed silence, and then an eruption of applause as the audience leapt to its feet.

Never mind that most weeks my piano books never came out of the car between lessons.

The most important part was the standing and the clapping. Over the years the actual image has changed, but the standing ovation has been the constant. By the time I met Larry, the image was more likely to be the congregation clapping after I preached at the Washington National Cathedral, even though that's never happened before there. There's a first for everything. And, anyway, it's my dream, and the people do what I want.

Or standing up and clapping when I completed my PhD, which no one did, not even my dissertation committee. They just shook my hand and went on with their gossip about the university's new president as if nothing out of the ordinary had just happened. I guess for them it hadn't.

Or winning an evangelism award (yes, there are those) for transforming a hundred-member congregation into North Carolina's first rural megachurch.

Now that I had moved to a place where I feared being forgotten, a place where no one was watching me, a place where people didn't even care if I had a PhD, a place where I was just a "preacher," I had managed to hijack a holy desire—the desire to deny myself—into a way to get noticed, to be remembered, to stay important. After all, people are still writing books about St. Francis and putting his statue in their flower gardens, aren't they?

"How should I let go? What should I release? How should I deny myself? Give away my books? Go on a fast? What should I give up? You're my spiritual director—help me craft a program of rigorous self-denial."

I could just see myself as I spoke—gaunt, joyful, holy. I could also see the people whispering as I walked by, admiring, marveling.

"Someone has said," Larry said after his usual moment of silence, "that when Jesus says 'deny yourself' he means 'deny your image of yourself.'"

---

This is probably as good a place as any to deal with one of the trickier issues that can't be avoided in the Christian life or in spiritual direction—obedience.

Obedience is out of fashion. In the same culture where God is expected to stay out of your way as you live your life, enjoy your liberty, and pursue your happiness, the idea of obedience isn't going to have many champions. When was the last time you heard a sermon on Paul's injunction for Christian husbands and wives to submit to one another and for wives to obey their husbands? When have you been to a wedding where anyone promised anyone else that they would, along with loving and honoring, also obey?

In our house we have a lot of parenting books. My parents are of the generation that parented the way their parents taught them to. I am of the generation that parents by the book. It's hard to find a parenting book that suggests the job of a parent has anything to do with teaching or expecting obedience. There seems to be one assumption they share in common: requiring obedience doesn't work. "Do it because I said so" is no more acceptable now that we are adults than we thought it was when we were children. Instead, we are encouraged to work with our children, to collaborate with them, to enter into win-win agreements in order to respect their dignity and autonomy as we help them discover the right way to behave.

There might even be people who think it's unethical to send dogs to obedience school. At least the schools don't call themselves obedience schools anymore.

When it's out of fashion for a spouse to obey, and it's discouraged to teach children to obey, and it's sketchy even to make dogs obey, what are we to do with stories from the Desert Fathers, with whom the tradition of Christian spiritual direction really begins? Stories like this one.

A hermit said, "Someone who hands over his soul in obedience to a spiritual guide has a greater reward than one who retires alone to a hermitage." He also said this: "One of the Fathers saw a vision of four ranks in heaven. The first rank was of those who are sick, yet give thanks to God. The second rank was of those who minister to the sick willingly and generously. The third rank was of those who live in the desert, seeing no one. The fourth rank was of those who for God's sake put themselves under obedience to spiritual guides. But those who live in obedience in the fourth rank wore necklaces and crowns of gold and shone more than the others." I said to the one who showed me the vision, "How is it that the rank which is lowest shines the most?" He replied, "Those who care for others do what they themselves want to do. Hermits follow their own will in withdrawing from the world. But the obedient have gone beyond their self-will, and depend only on God and the word of their spiritual guides: that is why they shine the most."

Obedience, this hermit says, is "the food of the saints who by its nourishment grow to fullness of life."

It's an enduring theme in the literature on spiritual direction: Submit your will to the will of the spiritual director. Obey. Even though there are traditions of spiritual guidance that stress the mutuality of the relationship, such as the Celtic tradition of the *anam cara*, soul-friend, or the medieval monk Aelred of Rievaulx's accent on spiritual friendship, the language of obedience and submission remains pervasive.

This question about obedience might be one of your chief questions if you've read any of this literature. You understand that entering into a relationship of spiritual direction means easing your grip on your supposed right of self-determination, but are you really expected in spiritual direction to let go completely of your own will and ability to make your own decisions? Will you have to obey blindly whatever your director says?

If the answer to these questions is yes, I suspect you might want to give up on the idea right now. Most people would.

You would have a difficult time finding a director who is willing to tell you what to do, I think, and that's because, while the notion of obedience has an important place in the Christian tradition of spiritual direction, it's understood in different ways.

When St. Benedict, the founder of Western monasticism, wrote the rule of life for his monks at Montecassino in the sixth century, he began with obedience.

Listen carefully, my son, to the master's instructions, and attend to them with the clear ear of your heart. This is advice from a father who loves you; welcome it, and faithfully put it into practice. The labor of obedience will bring you back to him from whom you had drifted through the sloth of disobedience. This message of mine is for you, then, if you are ready to give up your own will, once and for all, and armed with the strong and noble weapons of obedience to do battle for the true King, Christ the Lord.

As abbot, Benedict functioned as a kind of spiritual director for his monks, and he urged other abbots to treat monks gently and to know each one well. But he expected of the monks obedience. Still, there is a close connection between obedience and listening. The Latin words for "to listen" and "to obey" are closely linked in origin and meaning. Obedience, more than the act of "doing it now because I said so," requires listening attentively to the words of the director, not unlike the careful, attentive listening the director offers to you. Obedience is more about listening with the heart than blindly following directions. Episcopal priest and spiritual director Elizabeth Canham has said:

> The kind of listening Benedict calls for is a deep hearing that moves beyond understanding with the mind to a willingness for the heart to be moved. Because ear and heart are inextricably connected, obedience to God's call follows. ... The rote mouthing of prayers or doing of duty does not

constitute obedience; rather, open-hearted listening to God with a willingness to change equals obedience.

I suspect (spiritual directors, please correct me if I'm wrong) that most spiritual directors would not think their job is to tell the directee what to do, which doesn't mean there aren't a few who do so. But direction is not *directive* in that sense anymore. When it has been, as the nineteenth-century Roman Catholic spiritual director F. W. Faber warned, "The souls damaged by over-direction would fill a hospital in any large town."

When I hear Larry say something like, "To deny yourself means to deny your image of yourself," that is not a command. But I can obey nonetheless by listening deeply, open-heartedly, by letting go enough to make room for this word to work on me. We can obey by releasing the grip on our souls enough to let a word like this have the potential to shape us. Because the real point is this: the call we are meant to obey is God's.

In this conversation of spiritual direction, as Larry said to me the very first time we met, the Holy Spirit is the real director. What we are doing when we obey together, listening deeply to one another in the context of spiritual direction, is acting out our willingness to let a third Voice into the room, the ultimate authority, not one that speaks with the authority of a dictator—neither a good director nor God wants that kind of authority—but with the authority of an author whose words have the power to shape the story and the character of our lives.

When I release my stories in spiritual direction I am releasing the right to be the only author of my own life and opening myself to letting Larry's words be "obeyed," to sink from my ear to my heart so they might have a shaping influence over my story, all for the ultimate purpose of letting God's Spirit be the true author of my life.

Living in God's house of love as a good guest, I've learned through spiritual direction, means at least remembering that we didn't build this house but were invited into this life of God in which we live. And the shape of the house—its rooms, its walls, its colors, its doors—will shape the way we live. Practicing spiritual direction is one way of letting go of a sense of entitlement and learning to be a welcomed guest in our true home.

"Dreams of fame and fortune die hard, if they ever die at all," writes Frederick Buechner. God gave me an opportunity to let go of my dream, to let it die.

God gave me a chance to deny my image of myself—to obey.

I didn't like it at first.

I'd finished my dissertation, and it was time to turn it into a book. I was proud of the work I'd done, but the manuscript was doing me no good sitting in a box. I began to imagine that when it became a book it would liberate me from the obscurity of being a rural pastor. It would keep me from being forgotten. It would make me important.

I imagined walking into the bookstore in Raleigh where all my pastor friends shopped and seeing my book on the front display, a featured item. I imagined them inviting me to do a book signing. I imagined my bishop, the same one who sent me to the country, standing in line for my autograph. I nurtured this fantasy for some time.

To make it a reality, though, I'd have to get the right publisher. I had a list of publishers ranked in the order from highest to lowest in what I perceived to be their prestige. At the top of the list were the university presses at Oxford and

Cambridge. But they have the disadvantage of charging so much for books that they don't manage to sell very many. Next on the list was a publisher called Eerdmans, a non-denominational religious publishing house that publishes outstanding academic work and gets their books on bookstore shelves. Probably one-fourth of the books on my bookshelves were published by Eerdmans. After that, a few denominational publishing houses. And at the bottom of my list a press called Wipf and Stock. Not because they weren't publishing great things—they were. But they still had the reputation of being a publisher of mostly out-of-print books, even though they'd established a new imprint called Cascade Books that was publishing new academic books in theology. I had a friend who worked there. My advisor was influential in starting this press. Nothing but my own vanity put this publisher at the bottom of my list.

I thought through very carefully which publisher to submit the manuscript to first. I called old professors, who said, "If you ever want to get out of the country and teach at a seminary, send it to Eerdmans. They still have the best reputation."

That was good enough for me.

Why I decided to tell Larry about my reasoning process, I'll never know. I should have known better. But I told him how I decided to pick Eerdmans.

He listened attentively, as usual. Then he said three things.

First: "It seems like you have reasoned this out very carefully."

I thought his use of the word *reasoned* seemed suspicious. Was he suggesting there's another way to make these kinds of decisions?

Second: "We have a tendency to ask people for advice who we know will say what we want to hear."

I grant that. I didn't call my advisor because I knew he would tell me to send it to the press closest to his heart but at the bottom of my list.

And finally: "Did you ever think about asking God where to send it?"

*Why do I keep coming here?* I thought.

No, I hadn't asked God. That very week I had been reading Luke 9, meditating again on Jesus' command to "deny yourself." I'd underlined it in red during my devotional time that very morning. I was hoping God might ask me to deny myself by giving away our old red van.

If I had asked God, I was afraid he might have told me what I already knew—he didn't care much about my van but would be happy to invite me to give up my dream of fame and fortune instead by sacrificing my image of myself signing books.

I went home and held the copy of my dissertation. And I wept like a baby.

Then I e-mailed my friend at Cascade Books and asked him to send me their author guidelines. I told him I wanted them to publish my dissertation.

I didn't tell him I was doing it because God told me to. And I didn't tell him how much it hurt at the time. Waving goodbye to this dream of fame and fortune is one of the hardest things I've ever done.

The Quaker philosopher and writer Thomas Kelly describes exactly what was happening to me: "We are torn loose from earthly attachments and ambitions. . . . [God] plucks the world out of our hearts, loosening the chains of attachment."

God's plucking was teaching me to let go.

Three years later the doorbell rang. The UPS man had left a package on our doorstep. I brought the package inside, hunted for my pocket knife that was supposed to be in my pocket but wasn't, found it, and opened the package. Inside were five copies of a book called *The Shape of Participation: A Theology of Church Practices*. Beneath the title of the book there was a name. The name was mine.

I didn't glance out the window to see if a celebration parade was following the UPS truck, or if the neighbors were on their way over to see the book. I didn't sit by the phone and wait for the manager of that bookstore in Raleigh to call me. Why would I wait for a fantasy, a dream, one I had said goodbye to?

All I did was sit down and enjoy the moment. I held a copy in my hands and put the rest on the bookshelf. I enjoyed the feel of the smooth, shiny cover. I appreciated the work of the designer who designed the cover. I thought about the years of work that went into making this book— all the self-denials along the way, not just mine, but my wife's too. I sat there and enjoyed the feeling: satisfaction.

Satisfaction is only possible in the present. Dreams of fame and fortune make us restless. Learning to release them and stop living in a fantasy future was allowing me to live in the present. To be satisfied with life *now*, to pay attention to what God is doing *now*, to look around at all I have and all I don't have and say, "This is very good."

The publication of that book didn't change my life. But letting go of it three years earlier did. It made it possible for me to receive the book for what it is—the fruit of many years of hard work—without burdening it with the task of making me a famous somebody.

And it made it easier for me to pry my fingers off of unhealthy images of myself that distract me from God's presence in my life and from the love and beauty of this very moment.

# four

# Offering

I gave Larry a copy of my book because I don't pay him anything. I probably would have given him a copy anyway, but that doesn't change the fact that I don't pay him anything. I have given him small gifts, probably not more than three or four in the past five years. Fudge at Christmas, that kind of thing. If we were Old Testament people we'd probably call these thank-offerings, except there's no altar involved. I make a little offering every once in a while as a way of showing my gratitude.

You will find that some spiritual directors charge a fee and some don't. Sometimes a spiritual director is a priest or nun, supported by a parish or by his or her community—spiritual direction is a gift they can offer without needing payment. Some are on staff of a church, and spiritual direction is part of their ministry in that church. They get a salary, and they are expected to use their time this way. I recently heard of a spiritual director who is also a therapist. He charges for therapy, but not for spiritual direction. He gives his directees the name of a charity he supports and leaves it up to them if they want to make an offering to that charity as a way of saying thanks both to him and to God for this gift.

But there are some spiritual directors who work independently out of their homes or offices they rent. They do this work because they have discovered that God has given them a gift and called them to this ministry. They also know that God has not called them to stop eating. So they charge a slight fee, often on a sliding scale. It's likely that one of the first conversations you will have with a spiritual director is about discerning what is appropriate for you to pay.

Some people think it's a little strange to charge for spiritual direction. If this is a gift you have been given, how can you charge people to receive it?

But here's how I look at it. When I visit Larry, I think it's nice that the lights are on and we're not sitting in the dark. And that's because he's paid the electricity bill for his rented study. Speaking of study, it's also nice that he has this space. I suppose there are a few appropriate public spaces where someone could offer spiritual direction, but you would never know if someone is already sitting on your park bench before you get there. And what about when it rains?

It's also nice that Larry can afford to avail himself of opportunities for "professional development" so that he becomes increasingly better at using his gift.

And I'm guessing, unless severe fasting is one of his disciplines, Larry is a better, more attentive spiritual director when he's had a good breakfast. As far as I know, you still have to buy food.

I doubt that there are many spiritual directors who are using the fee to fund monthly trips to Vegas. It's nice to have a well-lit, dry, quiet space, with a director who's growing in his practice and whose stomach isn't growling.

That said, I don't pay Larry.

During our introductory visit Larry told me he charges on a sliding scale. "A seminary student who sees me pays twenty dollars. Others pay up to forty. You pray about it between now and our next visit, and we'll talk some more."

I did think about it, although I don't remember if I prayed about it. Cash flow in those days was tight, since my PhD stipend was coming to an end. So I arrived at our next visit a little anxious about how I could pay, and what I could pay, and whether I could continue.

I sat down. Larry spoke first.

"Since the last time we met," he said, "I've been praying, and I feel led not to charge you anything. So, if that's okay with you, you won't need to pay me a fee."

I said, "That would be okay. Thanks." Inside I was saying, "*Yippee!*"

---

I rarely give Larry a gift, and I never give him money. But I always make an offering. I offer my life—my stories and hopes, my dreams and fears, my anxieties and doubts. Sometimes my offering comes with tears rolling gently down my cheeks; sometimes it can be heard between bursts of laughter and the "yippee!" I've learned it's all right to say out loud. Other times the offerings slip out through a simple smile of gratitude.

However it comes out, I always make an offering because I know that whatever of me I offer in that room—whatever of me I am able to put on the table to view in the light of God's love and in the presence of one whose job it is to help me look at this life of mine in that way—is not being offered to Larry at all, but to God.

My stories, hopes, dreams, fears, anxieties, doubts—all that—on God's altar.

Whatever I offer here I am offering to God. And even though one hour a month isn't time to offer everything, it's practice in making my whole life an offering to the God who offered me this life to begin with.

---

We can receive the gift of spiritual guidance, which ultimately comes from God's own guiding Spirit but often in the company of a spiritual director, as we learn to see our lives as offering. And although what I'm talking about in this book are not stages or rigidly defined practices, it makes some sense that offering would come after releasing. We loosen our grip on our lives, and then we are able to offer them, to turn them into gift. The gift of our lives is not a gift to the spiritual director—it's a gift to God (given to us by God to begin with), but we make the offering tangible when we do it in the presence of another. This is what spiritual direction helps us to do. And this act of offering opens us to receive—to receive the gift of spiritual guidance from God's Spirit speaking, sometimes through the voice of another, more often from the depth of our own hearts.

There's an old word for this act of offering that I became reacquainted with a few years ago. I was at a retreat about seven hours away from my home. The retreat ended at noon on Saturday, and I still hadn't finished my sermon for the next day. (It's hard to write sermons when you're on spiritual formation retreats.) One of the others on the retreat had to leave early on Saturday, and since she lived close to me, I asked her if I could ride home with her. That way I'd have time to work on my sermon when I got home, but I'd also have to miss the speaker's last presentation. It seemed worth the sacrifice.

Until Saturday morning arrived. I wrestled with my sermon in my sleep, as I always do, and began to think, "Maybe I should stay and hear the presentation. Maybe there will be a word in it for me that will help me through this block." So I decided to stay. And indeed there was a word for me.

The presenter talked about learning to offer ourselves to God. He pointed us to pages 856 and 857 in the Episcopal Book of Common Prayer. There's a catechism in the back of that little black book with the translucent pages, and after you get through the Important Subjects in Capital Letters such as Creation, Sin, Redemption, Church—heady stuff if there ever was—the catechism turns to a series of questions about prayer and worship.

"What are the principal kinds of prayer?" it asks. And it answers: "The principal kinds of prayer are adoration, praise, thanksgiving, penitence, oblation, intercession, and petition." And it was "oblation" that caught my attention. A little later the catechism asks, "What is the prayer of oblation?" And it answers: "Oblation is an offering of ourselves, our lives and labors, in union with Christ, for the purposes of God."

That was the word I was waiting for: *oblation*—the offering of ourselves, our lives and labors (that means, I think, everything), in union with Christ (the only way Christians can offer themselves), for the purposes of God. And even though the catechism lists a number of principal types of prayer, I'm feeling bold enough to suggest that oblation is more principal than the rest (all kinds of prayer are equal, but oblation is more equal), because that simple definition sums up the goal of the Christian life: to offer our whole selves—mind, body, soul, spirit, and any other part of us you care to add to the list—our being and our doing, our speaking and our listening, our achieving and our failing—in union with Christ for the glory of God and God's purposes.

Not a bad definition of prayer itself, and the shape of a life that has become prayer. And it's a way of living and praying that makes it possible to receive spiritual direction. As St. Francis said, it is in giving that we receive. For how can we learn to see the gracious activity of God in our lives— the very thing we are hoping to do through the practice of spiritual direction—until we've made an offering of those very lives to the God already at work in them?

And so we practice this kind of prayer, and consequently this kind of life, sitting on the sofa, in the study, with that candle lit. When I tell my stories and Larry does all that he does, which is way more active than it looks if you just happened to peek in and see him sitting there—the listening, and accepting, and reflecting, and reminding, and encouraging, all with his hands resting gently in his lap and his stocking-footed feet motionless on the floor—I am making my oblation, putting my life on the table, on God's altar, saying: "Here, God, here is my life laid bare before you."

And more often than not, I could add: "Help me see where you are in this mess."

---

Often it feels as if all we have to offer is a mess—broken fragments of a life, rough and sharp-edged shards, which probably ought to be thrown away before anyone sees them—certainly not dragged into the light of day, not shown to a friend, not even a spiritual friend, and especially not to God. What could God possibly do with these fragments—with this mess?

As I write this it's December and the invitations to Christmas parties are going around. When you call someone to accept an invitation to a party, what's the first thing you say? *Can I bring anything?* We think we are saying that because we want to be helpful. But I think we really can't bear to show up empty-handed—just us. That wouldn't be good enough. "Oh, don't bring a thing," says the voice on the other end. "We have everything taken care of. Just bring yourself."

Who would ever let that happen? So you stop by the store on the way to the party, buy a bottle of wine with a fancy label, and slip it into one of those reusable wine bags, probably one of those someone brought you the last time you had a party. And when you arrive at the house, the host opens the door, and you smile and hold the bag out and say, "I know you said don't bring anything, but we just brought a little something."

Because behind the bottle of wine in that bag and behind that smile is, well, just you. And who could bear to show up with just *that?*

One of the fundamental moves we learn as part of the Christian life, and we practice it every time we offer one of our stories in spiritual direction, is how to show up to God's house empty-handed, with nothing to hold out in front of us to deflect attention from the pile of fragments that is our messy life. Nothing to hide behind.

"Just bring yourself," God says, "I've taken care of all the rest."

But Lord, if I just bring myself, all I have to offer is this quivering mass of fear and doubt and anxiety (and, if I'm honest, love and hope) and regret and . . .

"Great," God says. "That's all I want."

---

Offering God the blemished parts is hard to do. No fake smile and no store-bought gifts between me and the light of God's love. Not only do I not want to see this mess I have to offer, but I can't imagine anyone else, including God, would want to see it either.

Where in our culture do we have the safe space to offer even our worst, where that offering will not be rejected? At church? Not at many. At work? Certainly not. And that might be the reason you are longing for a spiritual director (or have already found one), because you've heard someone say, "It's one place I can offer everything without fear." And what we learn to offer here, we learn to offer to God as well.

But that doesn't mean offering isn't hard and doesn't hurt. Especially when it's that part of your life you'd like to keep hidden behind closed blinds. Especially when its one of the seven deadly sins.

There are few things I love more than playing with my boys. And there are few things that can provoke me to anger more quickly than my boys, especially my older boy when he was two.

Now I don't even remember what it was that made me mad, and I don't really want to look in my journal to remind myself. It could have been any number of things, but I do remember it was around bedtime, as usual, and Ginger was out of town. I had been busy with the boys all day and was looking forward to a quiet evening of reading after they went to bed.

And then a switch flipped in Simeon. It's as if he had a button that when pressed made him incapable of listening, being still, being quiet, following anything like direction, and why sometimes the switch got flipped and sometimes it didn't we never understood. But this night, when I was tired and home alone with them, it got switched, and I couldn't handle it.

I, apparently, have a switch, too. It seems to have been connected somehow to Simeon's because it usually got flipped shortly after his.

And all I really remember now was our big two-year-old sitting in the middle of an oversized sectional couch, with only his diaper on, and my red, hot, loud face, a foot from his, screaming.

I don't remember exactly what I was screaming, but there's a good chance it was something like this:

"What's wrong with you? Why can't you sit quietly for once? Why can't you stay in your bed? Why can't you leave your brother alone? Do you hear me? What's wrong with you?"

That there might be something wrong with him was not an infrequent suggestion in my angry rants.

And then he cried, and I was satisfied.

Somehow, I finally got him to bed. Then I went back into the family room and collapsed in the green recliner, the same chair I had rocked him to sleep in since he was two days old. I cried, and I began to say to myself in a kind of mantra, "You worthless father. What's wrong with *you*?"

That there might be something wrong with me was not an infrequent suggestion in my postanger meltdowns.

—————

In what kind of space could I make an offering of that story, of this pathetic life of mine? Who could accept it? Who could accept me? What God wouldn't throw me out of the house for that kind of behavior?

Somehow Larry had made the space, and not just with the couch and the candle and pictures on the wall. It was a space for my soul that his gentle, caring spirit had created. The space he had given me to screw up my courage and offer a story like this, which seemed beyond the pale. To offer it not because I wanted to, but because I had to.

Margaret Guenther, a spiritual director and teacher of spiritual direction, compares offering spiritual direction to offering hospitality. She says that one thing she offers when she offers true hospitality is the space for people to do their laundry. You would never let someone stay in your home but require them to leave their dirty laundry in their car.

No, you let them bring their dirty laundry in the house and wash it, underwear and all.

That's the kind of space a spiritual director creates, through the physical arrangement of the space, but also through her or his presence and listening.

We live most of our lives in places where only some of our life is welcomed, where we are welcomed if we come in our clean clothes. Many people come to church believing they have to wear their cleanest clothes. Leave the dirty stuff at home, please. Leave the arguments, the doubts, the fears. Leave the anxiety and the anger and the lust and the addictions. (In many churches, the addictions are allowed, but only in the middle of the week at the AA meeting in the basement. Please, no addictions on Sunday morning.) In fact, you might be better just staying home until you can get the mess of your life cleaned up.

And there are other clean-clothes places: Work, school, maybe even our own homes.

Most of us are not likely to have the kind of space for our souls that Parker Palmer calls a "circle of trust"—a place where the shy soul feels safe to speak, safe from mean-spirited and sometimes downright nosy questioning;

safe from judgment; safe to speak its truth without being rejected.

Safe to make an offering of itself, its *whole* self.

And when we don't experience that kind of space in our day-to-day lives, what is there to make us think being a guest in God's house is going to be any different? Can we offer our whole selves there, or should we leave the dirty clothes in the car? Maybe we should wash them down the road at the laundromat and come back when they're clean. After all, the Psalm says, "Who may abide in your tent? Who may dwell on your holy hill? Those who walk blamelessly and do what is right." That's not me, at least not when I'm angry.

But a spiritual director creates that circle of trust, that place where it is safe for us to offer our whole selves without fear of judgment. And when you get in the habit of making such offerings in this space, whether it's an office, a house, or a church, and when you learn that however ugly your offering seems to you, you will still be invited back next month, that's called training—training in getting more comfortable with the idea that we can offer our whole lives to God as well.

That God's house of love has a laundry room, and we're welcome to use it.

---

God says the same thing to all of us that Larry said to me when I told him the story of my anger with Simeon and my self-loathing. I know God says the same thing Larry said, because Larry was only quoting what God had already said long ago.

"Roger, I do not condemn you."

In the silence that followed tears ran down my cheeks.

"It's hard to share these difficult stories about ourselves, isn't it?"

"That's not why I'm crying."

"Why then?"

"Because I'm not condemned."

I took a risk making this offering. And it wasn't rejected.

St. Francis was right. It *is* in giving that we receive. Even if what we have to give isn't so fine.

---

The early Desert Fathers warned not to hide anything from your spiritual father. Tell him all your thoughts, they said. Offer everything; hold nothing back.

But here's one thing I've discovered: that's impossible. In the course of a month I have many thoughts, experiences, fears, and hopes, 90 percent of which I'm sure I don't remember. And although each one of these thoughts, feelings, experiences, fears, hopes, and anxieties is appropriate to bring to spiritual direction—it's about our whole lives with God, after all—there simply isn't time in one hour to share them all.

How do you decide what to offer?

Or, to put the question in the more pedestrian way I ask myself each month: *What am I going to talk to Larry about this time?*

It's probably a mistake to drive to your appointment each month with a firm list in hand of the three things you want to talk about. You need to leave room for the Spirit to move even at the last minute, to bring something to mind that might be just the right thing to offer that day. I can remember a few times leaving Larry's office and saying, "This wasn't what I had planned to talk about, but it was the right thing."

Don't show up with an agenda. But don't show up unprepared, either.

In my experience, it's useful to give some time, thought, and prayer to what you will bring to spiritual direction. And this is where some silence and a pen and a journal can be very helpful.

The day or so before your meeting with your spiritual director, you can do something like the Jesuit practice of the daily examen recommended by St. Ignatius. The daily examen is a practice of prayer that invites you to look back over the previous twenty-four hours and ask where you sensed God's presence or absence; where you felt afraid or anxious; where you were at peace; where you needed God's help.

I suggest that you do this looking back over the month. Ask yourself: Where was God's presence palpable for me this month? Where was God's absence palpable? What fears and anxieties, or hopes and dreams, kept me from being attentive to God in my daily life? For what do I have to be thankful this month? When did I fail to give thanks? Why?

Writing about these things can bring events and moments in our lives, hidden beneath waves of busyness, back to the surface where we can examine them in God's light. You might just discover one or two moments it would be worth offering in spiritual direction. After a while, you will have your own list of questions you have found helpful to ask as you prepare for spiritual direction.

There is one final question to ask. You don't need to ask it every month, but ask it on occasion: Is there something—a secret of some sort, a particular fear or anxiety or experience—that I'm avoiding telling my spiritual director, or anyone else for that matter?

If the relationship with your spiritual director is new, this might not be the place to begin. But if after months or even years you find consistently that there is a something you are avoiding talking about (something like one of the so-called seven deadly sins), it might be helpful to be explicit with yourself and ask: What exactly is it I don't want to say, and why?

We want to live in God's house of love. But we will never be able to do it, and enjoy living there and relax, as long as we have left the bag of dirty laundry in the trunk of the car, the drawstring of the bag pulled so tight not even a sock can fall out.

The good new is: God is patient. And if your spiritual director is a good one, he or she is patient as well. I know mine is. So I have all the time in the world to share what I need to share, to offer what I need to offer, and to receive whatever blessing God has for me through this relationship.

---

Once I gave Larry baseball cards.

I'd been home to visit my mom and dad, and Mom reminded me that there's a lot of stuff in the house that belongs to me from years ago—trophies from band competitions, letters from old girlfriends, boxes of college term papers, a collection of coins given over fifteen Christmases by my grandmother, and thousands of baseball cards I collected between the fourth and eighth grades. I told her she could throw out the trophies and the letters. We drove home with the coins and the cards.

I hadn't looked through those cards in more than twenty years. I enjoyed most looking through the binder of my favorites, most of them players for the Cubs in the 1980s. I had about fifty different cards of the Cubs' second baseman, number 23, Ryne Sandberg. And just looking at these cards reminded me of days I had long forgotten, lazy Saturdays with my brother and our next-door neighbor Chris McRoberts, sitting on the floor in our living room, organizing and counting and trading cards. And trips to the flea market in Louisville where we bought cards to add to our collections.

I have known for some time that Larry is a baseball card collector. I suspect his collection is much larger than mine, since he's in his seventies and still doing it. He told me once he buys a pack when he goes to the drugstore, and not for the gum.

So for Christmas one year I got out my cards and started flipping through them, intending to give a few to Larry. I had some packs from twenty-five years ago that were unopened. That will be a nice surprise, I thought. A few Boston Red Sox cards for a Red Sox fan. And even a Ryne Sandberg, which I would have never given away without a handsome exchange. Out of thousands of cards, I found just the right few.

There's not time in one hour a month, or one hour a day for that matter, to offer all of our stories. But if we take the time to think about our lives and flip through the binder of our stories, we might find just the right ones—the ones that will show us where and what God is up to, or the ones that will help us see how little we know about where and what God is up to, and how that can be okay sometimes.

And perhaps a story we never would have parted with years ago. But now, the Spirit seems to be saying, is the right time to offer it.

And just as I watched Larry unwrap that twenty-five-year-old pack of cards, we also might find that, right there in that room, we unwrap surprises, a long-forgotten moment we hadn't thought of in years but seems just right now. And we are surprised and our director is surprised and God is delighted, because surprises are one of the things God likes best.

So go ahead, offer it.

# five

# Trusting

Finally, it was my turn. After two years of Ginger's being gone for five days every three months on a spiritual retreat called the Academy for Spiritual Formation; two years of watching her come back glowing and refreshed, telling stories about the movement of the Spirit in her life, about the silence, the long walks around the lake, the community worship she didn't have to plan or lead, and the meals she didn't have to make or clean up after; two years of being home alone with two toddlers so Ginger could go away and learn to be spiritual; two years of watching her drive away and wishing I were away somewhere being spiritual too;

two years of reading the books for *her* spiritual formation program but never getting the real experience myself; two years of being a sidelined spectator to Ginger's growth in her life of prayer—after two years it was finally my turn.

There was really one reason I wanted to go to this two-year academy for spiritual formation. It wasn't for the book learning. I'd already read Ginger's books and had had enough book learning. Anyway, Ginger bought the CDs of her lecturers, so I could listen to them in the car. That's not what I wanted.

I wanted one thing—the silence.

I wanted that room to myself that I could retreat to after evening prayer while someone else five hundred miles away was putting the boys to bed, the room where I could read and pray and write and sleep and could feel confident that no little person in footed pajamas would walk in and throw up on me, or smile even, or need to be put back in bed forty times, or do anything else to interrupt my solitude. I wanted the hours with my journal or my book, time to listen to God, and, just in case Paula D'Arcy is right that "God comes to you disguised as your life," time to look at and listen to my own life as well, because in my life as husband, father, pastor, and student finishing a doctoral dissertation, I didn't have much time to listen to God or look at my life—which turn out to be remarkably similar activities.

So when Ginger was about to finish her two-year academy, I signed up for one. Mine would begin in October; hers would end in November. On the first Sunday of October, after worship, I would drive to Holy Trinity, a monastery outside of Baltimore, and the monkish soul inside of me would finally have some peace and quiet.

———

These are exactly the kinds of things you talk about in spiritual direction—the things you are longing for. Maybe you have a monkish soul like mine, or maybe yours is more extroverted. Either way, what is it crying for? What are you wanting, hoping, longing for?

So I shared with Larry my process of deciding to sign up for the academy and also my joy when the time of departure was drawing near.

I would leave after church on Homecoming Sunday— always the first Sunday of October, and always the largest crowd in church except for Easter Sunday, and by far the best meal of the year. I'd stay long enough to eat my share and get some of Mrs. Walters' chocolate cake, and then I'd drive off. Off to my monastery for a week. Off to my silence.

I shared this with Larry—my enthusiasm, my hopes, my longing to enter the silent land. How I wished for it! Indeed, I was desperate for it. And he could tell. In fact, it reminded him of something he'd heard me say before.

I suspect all good spiritual directors do this—help you make connections between your stories, connections you might not make precisely because they are yours. You are so close to them you can't see the big picture. Listening to myself tell a story is like standing a foot away from Monet's *Water Lilies* and forgetting that this lily pad in front of my face looks remarkably like the others. I'm simply too close to notice. Maybe God does come to you disguised as your life. All the more reason we need someone else looking at our lives with us, objective enough to see the broader patterns.

Larry's not too close to my life. In his chair a few feet across the room, he's at the perfect distance to help me see it more broadly.

"You know what your longing for silence reminds me of?"

I didn't know. I don't remember if I said I didn't know, or if I just let the blank look on my face answer for me.

"It reminds me of the time you talked about becoming so angry with Simeon, often during those very weeks Ginger was away. That anger happened most in the evenings when his behavior got in the way of your quiet evening that you'd been looking forward to all day long."

This time the expression on my face said, yep, you remember rightly.

"I hear that same sense of longing as you talk about going to the academy. But what happens if it's not what you expect? What if you are disappointed? How will you respond?"

He was asking me exactly the right question. He wasn't suggesting that my wanting silence was wrong but encouraging me to think whether my desperate desire for silence might be setting me up for disappointment. For some time we'd been talking about the importance of letting go, of releasing, in receiving spiritual direction and in our lives with God altogether, and here was another place Larry was inviting me to let go—to release my narrow expectations so I would be open to receive whatever it was *God* had for me during my time away.

If you have your heart set on one thing, and one thing alone—in my case, silence in solitude—how will you be able to recognize and receive God's interruptions when they come in surprising ways? Will you respond in openness, or like a dad whose child has ruined his quiet evening?

The word Larry next used was a classic religious word for what comes after letting go and opening to God's interruptions. It was a verifiable church word, but he helped me see it in a new way.

"Instead of going to your first week of retreat with clear expectations of what you want and need, why don't you take some time this week and prepare yourself to *trust*—prepare yourself to be able to receive graciously God's gracious interruptions?"

Trust.

———

I was already learning that trust is one of the dispositions that makes receiving spiritual direction possible.

When I took our son Silas to his prekindergarten doctor's appointment for the required four vaccinations, the doctor asked him a number of questions, such as: Do you eat breakfast? Is there a gun in your house? Can you read? Do you know how to swim? Silas did great on all the questions but the last one. He didn't know how to swim, and he told her so, with a furtive glance in my direction.

Dr. G. (her last name is too hard to pronounce or spell) is not the doctor we usually see. We usually see the affable Dr. Clark, who does a remarkable job at making us inept and inexperienced parents feel as though we're doing a great job and there's nothing to worry about. Dr. G. had a different approach—glare at you with piercing eyes and make you feel like a wretch of a parent in order to shame you into doing a better job. A month earlier I'd gotten the lecture about healthy eating when she discovered our older son's body mass index was too high for a seven-year-old. And I felt another one coming on, this time about the importance of learning to swim.

But it was mercifully short and actually had a useful point—even if he doesn't learn how to swim this summer ("which you would teach him to do if you cared about his safety"), at least teach him to float. A child who knows how to float will be safer and more confident in the water.

That didn't sound too hard.

But teaching a tentative child to float is easier said than done. You support him with your arms as he lies back in the water. You remind him to keep his head back, not to have his chin pinned against his chest, and to keep his belly up. And he might do this while your arms are beneath him, because he's learned to trust your arms over the years. But as soon as you say you're going to move your arms, and you begin slowly to slide them from beneath his back, his head pops up, his butt goes down, and he starts to sink. And you have to grab him and pull him up.

At this point, I suggest getting out of the pool and having some snacks.

The object is to get the child to trust the water to buoy him. But first he has to trust *you*.

The object of spiritual direction is learning to trust yourself to God's grace in all things—God's supporting, loving, buoying grace. If you haven't done this before, it's not so easy. As soon as we doubt whether we're actually being held, we begin to work ourselves, trying to keep ourselves afloat in this pool called life, and that doesn't work so well.

Learning a life of prayer is like learning to float in God's love. It helps to have a good guide, who has done it before and shown others how.

I had been learning to trust Larry.

---

The story of two sixteenth-century saints illustrates the importance of having a spiritual guide one can trust.

Teresa of Ávila is known as one of the great mystics in Christian history, whose experiences of God were profound and sometimes alarming. She was nothing like the stereotypical nun—cloistered, silent, contemplative. An active woman to the end, she spent the last ten years of her life founding convents throughout Spain in an effort to restore the Carmelite order to its original simplicity and austerity.

But this didn't keep God from granting her what she called "favors"—ecstatic experiences of his love that were both delightful and painful. Many times she was nearly paralyzed during these experiences, these raptures, and many people wondered if they were really from God, not least being Teresa herself. At the height of the Spanish Inquisition, you couldn't be too safe making sure your spiritual experiences were within the bounds of orthodoxy. Teresa herself was prone to doubt them. She constantly feared that the devil was playing tricks on her. As much as she reflected on her own experience, she couldn't be sure they were from God.

So she sought wise guides she could trust—in that culture, always men. She sought men of learning and experience. (She had a very difficult time finding them.) She often found men of learning but who themselves had such shallow lives of prayer they were only frightened when they heard her recount her experiences. And she sometimes found men of prayer but who were so shallow intellectually they couldn't help or discern whether her experiences were orthodox.

Over the years she found a few. One of them was the other great sixteenth-century mystic, St. John of the Cross. Temperamentally, the two couldn't have been more opposite. Teresa was talkative and outgoing, even jolly, and sometimes irreverent; John was quiet, small, introverted, somber. But both of them had souls yearning to float in God's love, and John, with his learning, was able to put these experiences in the theological context of God's gracious working in the soul. And he himself knew the importance of having a spiritual guide you can trust. Because when you start going through a dark night—that period in the spiritual life when previous experience and the senses become useless in helping you find your way forward, and "favors," the delightful experiences of God's presence, disappear—you enter a wilderness, a place of disorientation. Without a guide you trust, who can tell you to keep going because there's nothing to fear, and who can help you know what to *do* to keep going, you are likely to turn around and run, according to John—back to earlier ways of praying, active ways of praying with the mind, ways that are more like swimming than floating. But at least you're in control then.

In the dark night, God is teaching you to float, but you'll likely be too afraid to learn without a spiritual guide.

Teresa and John were these guides for each other. The culture of the day demanded a hierarchy. Even though John was much younger than Teresa and became a friar in Teresa's movement of reform, because he was a man he was supposed to be her superior. She brought him for a time to the convent where she was the prioress in order to be the confessor for the nuns there as well as for herself.

But the nuns testified that at night Teresa and John were often seen in intense spiritual conversation, during which they would be levitating in their chairs as they spoke. Clearly, they trusted each other as spiritual friends. And because of that trust, they were learning to let God buoy them. They were learning to float.

---

There are no shortcuts. Learning trust in the relationship of spiritual direction, as in any relationship, takes time.

But I can make one suggestion that I think will create the space for real trust to grow, trust that will be mutual. After you've gone through the process of finding a spiritual director—of praying, and searching, and asking, and meeting with two or three—and after you've found one you think you might establish a relationship with (the feeling, one hopes, will be mutual), then make a promise to yourself: I'm going to stick with this. I'm going to stick with *him* or *her*. I'm going to see this through.

Now, there's no way to know what that means in advance. But you might give yourself a year. You might say to yourself, I don't know what's going to happen in this relationship, or where or how God is going to show up or where God is going to lead me. But I know this is important, and I know this is what I need, and so I'm not going to consider getting another spiritual director.

Maybe you don't need to set a specific time. But have a resolution in your heart. *I'm going to stick with this.*

The Desert Fathers and Mothers knew that we humans are restless. That's why when Anthony the Great was asked what one should do in order to please God, he replied, "Wherever you go, keep God in mind; whatever you do, follow the example of holy Scripture; wherever you are, stay there and do not move away in a hurry."

They knew that as soon as something doesn't seem to be "working" for us anymore, we'll want something else to do. As soon as a place doesn't seem to be the place where we feel God or where God is speaking to us or where we get warm spiritual fuzzies, we'll pack our bags and go looking for new warm fuzzies someplace else.

Growth in trust requires taming this restlessness.

A few weeks ago a woman visited our church. She was a member of the church in town where my wife had been an associate pastor six years earlier. She said she might start coming more often because the personnel committee at her church had done some things she hadn't liked, and the choir had also done some things she hadn't liked. I wanted to be hospitable, so I told her she's always welcome here. But what I wanted to say was, "Chances are, the staff relations committee here will do something you don't like eventually, as will the choir. So you might as well just stay where you are."

We are always looking for greener pastures. And the temptation is the same in spiritual direction. As soon as we go through a dry period, or it seems as if we're not getting as much out of it, or our spiritual director has to do the rare and hard work of challenging us, our temptation is to want a change. *He doesn't understand me anymore. He's not as wise as I thought. I need someone else.*

And as long as we allow that possibility, we will never learn trust. Because trust can only flourish in the context of a commitment where the escape hatches are closed, where we have to learn to move forward together, trusting one another.

If you've closed the escape hatches but still begin to think this isn't the right relationship, or for whatever reason, you are having trouble growing in your trust, so that letting go and offering are increasingly difficult, before you go looking around for another spiritual director, there's one thing you need to do—say it. Make it part of your offering.

Say, "I'm struggling in this relationship. I don't know if you understand me. For whatever reason, I'm having a difficult time trusting you."

These might be some of the hardest things you've had to say. But if you are able to say them, I can tell you one thing—there is more trust there than you know.

———

Learning to trust your spiritual guide isn't an end in itself. It's a step on the way to trusting God.

When my wife and I manage to pray together, which isn't every day but is more often now than it was a year ago, we do it early in the morning. When our alarms go off at five—hers beeping loud enough I swear it's going to wake up the children, and mine tuned to National Public Radio—we hit the snooze button at least twice. But by 5:30, one of us, having gotten out of bed, nudges the other one on the shoulder and says something really spiritual like, "Well, we might as well pray."

So, trying not to trip over the baby gates at the top and bottom of the stairs, we shuffle downstairs to the kitchen, where, if we had planned ahead, hot coffee will be awaiting us. But since we're usually as tired at night as we are in the morning, too tired to fix the coffee and set the timer, the coffee isn't waiting. So Ginger starts gathering the books— the Book of Common Prayer to tell us which psalm to read, the Bible because it's got the psalms in it, and the *Upper Room Worshipbook*, because this has the order for morning prayer we like—and I start making the coffee.

Once the coffee starts brewing we sit down, light a candle if one of us happens to think about it in the fog of morning, and open the prayer book. Our voices are raspy. Our eyes are only half-opened. If you have ever thought there is anything romantic or heroic about praying early in the morning, like David announcing in a psalm, "I will awaken the dawn"—perish the thought. It's just hard. Especially when the coffee's not ready.

And then something extraordinary happens. To the background music of coffee drip, drip, dripping in the pot, we say the opening words.

> God said: Let there be light; and there was light.
> And God saw that the light was good.
> This very day our God has acted! Let us rejoice!
> Alleluia! God's name be praised.

The coffee wasn't ready. The lights weren't on. The prayer books were not out. The baby gates were still closed. The sun had not started poking its rays through the pine trees in our backyard, and the birds hadn't even begun to sing, and yet *God has already acted*. How extraordinary!

It's as if every groggy morning is a little Easter. "Early on the first day of the week, while it was still dark, Mary Magdalene came to the tomb and saw that the stone had been removed." While she was sleeping, God was working. That very day, God had acted, before Mary showed up.

And that's the God we are learning to trust—the God who goes ahead of us.

We awake and stumble around. We are always moving into the future as if into an unknown. We don't know what's ahead of us. And the temptation is toward what Parker Palmer calls "functional atheism"—the belief that if something is going to happen it's our job to make it happen. I need to know what I want to accomplish today and plan accordingly, minimize interruptions, and make things turn out right.

For me, it might be: If I'm ever going to have a bit of silence tonight, I'd better figure out how to get these kids down early and keep them in bed. Because I know what I want and what I need and it's up to me to make it happen.

Functional atheism.

But trust says: God is already out front (what John Wesley called God's *prevenience*, God's going before). God is already at work. The coffee might not be there, but God already is. How would our lives look different if we walked into all the future minutes and days and weeks acknowledging the God who is already up ahead, already acting, already rolling away stones, already preparing surprises, the divine interruptions that are actually what we need?

And sometimes such a divine interruption is wearing footed pajamas.

As we learn trust in spiritual direction, our trusting one another is not an end in itself. In most relationships it is. In a friendship it is. In a marriage it is. But in spiritual direction it's more like trusting your dad to teach you to float. You trust him, because what you really want to learn is to trust the water.

And you trust your spiritual director, because, remember, you have discovered in your heart a longing—to trust

God, to learn to live in the house of love, a house you can't see or touch. A house you don't know your way around in. You want to learn to live surrounded by and attentive to God's grace, trusting the God who goes before you. You want to learn to trust that, as you move from room to room in your life, as you spend your days going up and down the stairs, sometimes in the light, more often in the dark, thinking and hoping you know what the next room holds, God is already there, getting the room ready, maybe not the way *you* would get the room ready, maybe with a few surprises, some for you to enjoy, some for you to puzzle over, some you will never understand.

When you bump into a door that won't open, you want to trust.

When you trip over a baby gate, you want to trust, because, as Psalm 37 says, "though we stumble, we shall not fall headlong, for the LORD holds us by the hand."

---

It was finally my turn. The lavish homecoming lunch wasn't over yet, but my soul was longing to be somewhere else. I kissed Ginger, kissed the kids, walked home from the church, put on comfortable driving clothes, and set off for Holy Trinity.

I still hoped for a little silence. But I had spent the week preparing in prayer for whatever God was preparing ahead of me. Part of that was practicing that other lesson I'd been learning all along—letting go. I spent the week letting go of my own narrow expectations. I was going forth with an attitude of trust.

What stones would I discover rolled away during my week of retreat? I was looking forward to being surprised.

I got to my room. Each of our rooms at Holy Trinity had a sink. There was a common men's restroom with showers at the end of the hall—but at least we had our own sink. I quickly learned two things: The fellow in the room next to me had a habit of compulsively washing his hands. At every hour of the day and night, I heard him turning on and off his faucet. When I tried to nap, he washed his hands. I prayed, he washed; I read, he washed. I was beginning to wonder if he was taking too literally Psalm 24, "Who shall ascend the hill of the LORD? And who shall stand in his holy place? Those who have clean hands and pure hearts."

He might also have had an unusually small bladder. I can't be sure. But I do know he left his room to walk around what seemed like every twenty minutes. Maybe he was going to the restroom, maybe somewhere else. And every time he left, the heavy wooden door slammed behind him, shaking my walls and echoing down the hall.

I prayed, slept, rested, and read to the tune of running water and slamming doors.

I wasn't surprised about this part, the ruined silence, nor was I dismayed. Somehow I was ready for it. And anyway, it was October in Maryland. There couldn't have been a more beautiful month. So I did find solitude and silence outside among the trees and the deer. That was a great blessing. I wasn't wrong to think I needed this. I did, and I'm glad I found it.

But I also found what I didn't know I needed—friends. I thought I was going on a retreat to escape people, and yet the relationships I made at that first retreat, and which lasted for two years, were the great surprise blessing. The stone God rolled away was the stone of my closed-off heart, and God opened it so I could discover the gift of others.

I thought I was walking into a room to be alone, alone with God, of course, but alone nonetheless. What I discovered was that God was already in the room, and he'd brought a lot of his friends. And because the room I had to be alone in was especially noisy, I had nothing better to do than to hang out in the room with God and his friends. This turned out to be the dining hall, with a great vaulted ceiling and big, round tables and plenty of food and good conversation to linger over.

Later in the week, when the retreat was almost over, and I was basking in the joy not of solitude—surprise!—but of company, I took a walk. I sat down on the trail, overlooking a wooded ravine. The ground was covered with golden leaves and the trees were half-bare. The wind was blowing, so I sat and watched leaf after leaf let go of its branch and float to the ground to join the others. And these leaves became parables for me. How much, I imagined, a leaf must trust to let go and descend, not knowing how far it is to the ground, or where it will land. Simply letting go, and trusting, and floating on the currents of the air.

I thought: that's what I want to do.

And then I thought: that's what I *am* doing.

And, finally, I thought: I can't wait to talk to Larry about this.

# six

# Attending

The phone call was the second event in a span of three days that began the process of our deciding it was time to leave the small church where we'd been the pastors for two and a half years. Talking with Larry was the third.

It was my friend Craig who called. Craig was a seminary classmate of ours and was a groomsman in our wedding. It was not unusual for him to call, but most of the time when he got in touch there was something specific he wanted to talk about. So after chatting about how things were going, he finally got to the point.

"You know Sally Trent in Charlotte?"

Indeed I did. When Ginger was an associate pastor we had used one of her books with a study group. She was the pastor of one of the largest Methodist churches in that part of the state, a great preacher, and a prolific writer.

"Sally is looking to add one or two people to the staff of her church. One of them would focus on Christian formation for young adults. Apparently someone mentioned your names to her. She called me to ask if I knew you and thought you'd be interested. I told her I did know you and that I would give you a call and feel you out."

Going to a different church was the farthest thing from my mind. I had developed an almost heroic determination to stick it out in the country. Wasn't this part of my spiritual growth, learning to stay and work in a place where I might be forgotten? Where I wouldn't get recognition? I was trying to learn to let go of the idea of working in big churches in big cities. Furthermore, in the past fifty years the average pastoral tenure at our church was two and a half years, and I'd been here long enough to know that these people deserved better than that. They deserved commitment. I was sure I was the one. I was trying to learn what those desert monks called stability.

And then there was the building project. I'd spent the last two years talking to architects and contractors and raising money to build a new fellowship hall and to make our entire building handicap-accessible. This work had captivated my imagination, and in a few months we would finally start building, after long years of dreaming, discussing, and praying. It seemed as if there couldn't have been a worse time to leave. As one of those desert monks said, "If someone lives in a place but does not harvest the crops there, the place will drive that person out for not having done the work of that place." We'd been planting and watering, and I wasn't going to leave before the harvest came in.

I told Craig this, but I also said something that surprised me, but which I instantly knew was true. "I'm not prepared to leave yet, but I think Ginger would go tomorrow. She has real gifts and passion for the work of Christian formation with young adults, and in this setting she hardly gets to do any of that. She misses it, and I think she'd jump at the chance to devote herself full-time to that kind of work."

We ended the conversation agreeing that the pastor could get in touch with us and tell us more about what she's looking for. I told Ginger about the conversation, and she did see an opportunity to do the kind of work she longed to do. I was still determined we would stay, but the door I kept shut was now ajar.

I had an appointment with Larry the next day—just in time to talk through some of these issues. And especially to talk through what had happened the previous Sunday morning (the first event), when I showed such remarkable self-restraint that I didn't scream at my children's Sunday school teacher.

I've said that when going to spiritual direction, you shouldn't have a agenda set in stone, but you shouldn't go unprepared either. You should arrive with what you might call prepared flexibility, some ideas of what you want to talk about coupled with a willingness to let the Holy Spirit lead you in a different direction.

But then there are those times when you know *exactly* what you need to talk about, and you're sure the Spirit wouldn't dare change your mind. And what I needed to talk about was my anger again, but not at my children this time—this time at a church member. Anger I had wisely managed not to let rise as high as my lips, but I wasn't sure how much longer I could keep it down.

"And pay attention to your family. Don't be blind to their needs. Has your determination to stay kept you from listening to your wife's soul—her longing to use her gifts and to be fulfilled in her ministry? Has it kept you deaf to your children? Given what you described about their Sunday school, are you in touch enough with them to know if their spirits are flourishing? I'm giving you a warning— pay attention to your soul, pay attention to your wife, pay attention to your children. There's no way to pay attention to God if you don't pay attention to yourself and those closest to you. Don't let heroic fantasies blind you."

He gave me a word, all right—pay attention. And it was the word I needed to hear.

I'd been angry. I'd answered the phone call from Craig. And I'd received a warning. It was time to take notice—to attend.

---

What if God does come to you disguised as your life? What if God comes to me disguised as the angry, ambitious, God-longing, funny, slightly overweight husband, father, pastor—human being—that I am? For most of us that would be a frightening thought, because our lives are so filled and preoccupied that we hardly have the time, the space, or the inclination to pay attention to this particular human life we are living right now. But if I'm going to learn to live my life self-consciously in the home that is God's love, and let that home shape me, I'm going to have to learn to pay attention, because it's me, after all, and not someone else who is doing the living of my life. It would be a shame to miss it.

And the only time we can live in God's house is now. We can't live with God yesterday—that's past—and we can't live with God tomorrow—because that's, well, tomorrow. But we can live with God *now*. And that means learning to be attentive to the life that is right in front of us and all around us, the people and places and bits of work and fears and desires that together form the constellation of the present moment. And your constellation is different from mine. So pay attention.

In his wonderful little book *Making All Things New*, Henri Nouwen suggests what keeps us from paying attention to the stars that make the constellation of the present moment: fearful preoccupations, otherwise known as worry. "Our individual as well as communal lives are so deeply molded by our worries about tomorrow that today hardly can be experienced."

And I would add: not just worries about tomorrow, but also regret about the past, and painful memories, and self-dramatizing fantasies about the future. We spend such enormous amounts of soul-energy fretting about the past, worrying about the future, or dreaming about a better day that we miss what is going on right under our noses—the anxiety of a child, the heart-stirrings of a spouse, the anger that's just beginning to course through our own veins—until it's too late.

We need a warning: pay attention.

And we might need it from a spiritual director whose job it is to direct our attention again and again back to the present, back to our own lives, away from the rabbits we chase and the anxious distractions, and to what God might be saying to us now.

But even if you don't have a spiritual director, you've already gotten this warning from the best spiritual director of all.

"I tell you, do not worry about your life, what you will eat or what you will drink, or about your body, what you will wear. Is not life more than food, and the body more than clothing? Look at the birds of the air; they neither sow nor reap nor gather into barns, and yet your heavenly Father feeds them. . . . Consider the lilies of the field, how they grow; they neither toil nor spin. . . . So do not worry about tomorrow, for tomorrow will bring worries of its own. Today's trouble is enough for today."

This is a warning from someone who, with a cross looming in his future, had plenty to worry about. And yet he gives advice about worry that has been turned into an old, worn-out cliché: stop and smell the roses.

I've spent a lot of time thinking about this passage, perhaps because I am congenitally (and perhaps habitually) anxious. And I have come to believe that Jesus' command to "look at the birds" and "consider the lilies" is more than just an illustration to show how God takes care of God's creatures. I think Jesus is actually saying: If there is a bird in front of you, look at it, learn from it. That is your present. If you are passing a field of wildflowers, consider them. Meditate on them. Learn from them. They are your present. The way to banish worries is not to engage in mental jihad with them, as if they are rebels occupying your mind and you must rout them. The way to get rid of worries is to pay attention to the present. Give yourself fully to what is in front of you.

But Jesus' command goes deeper than simple advice on how to get rid of worry, even though that's useful. There is a divine element here as well. The reason we pay attention to today and stop worrying about tomorrow is that *today is the only place we can encounter God*. Looking at the birds is training in paying attention to God's activity in the present, which is the only place we can experience God's activity. Considering the lilies is training in attending to God.

Maybe Jesus should have added: Consider your life. For there, if we pay attention, we might hear God speak as well.

———

It was an ancient Greek philosopher, Socrates, who said, "Know thyself." But Christian theologians throughout the centuries have said that knowledge of God and knowledge of self go hand in hand. Self-knowledge, for Christians, is not an end in itself. Self-knowledge is one of the ways we come to know God.

St. Augustine, the great bishop and theologian, who has taught us more about desire and its twisted potential than anyone else, went on a search for God. His search took him through many turns until, having received spiritual guidance from Christian friends, from the preaching of St. Ambrose, and from his own reading of Scripture, he made a profound discovery—he'd been off searching for God, but God was there all the time. He didn't have to go anywhere to find God. For, as he discovered, God was closer to him than he was to himself.

If he's right, then maybe paying attention to those selves to whom God is inexpressibly close is one way to find God.

A few weeks ago my family was having dinner with some friends. The wife of the couple teaches New Testament at a nearby seminary. They are very happy. Their children go to a fine school. She has tenure. They just bought a new house and are finished with the burden of unpacking. They are feeling more settled than they have ever felt before.

And then she did what I had done—she answered the phone.

While we were eating dinner she told us about the call. It was from the dean of another seminary, a slightly more conservative one on the theological spectrum, and our friend is one of the more conservative members on the theological spectrum of her own seminary faculty. For instance, she is willing to argue that Paul wrote the letter to the Ephesians and that the Gospel of John is a trustworthy account of the life of Christ, both of which run against the grain of more liberal academic orthodoxies. The dean of this other seminary was inviting her to apply for a position there. She would fit in better. She would probably get a raise, maybe an endowed chair. She'd certainly be made a full professor.

But they'd also have to leave all the things that made their life so rewarding. Her husband's job was turning a corner, and he was for the first time in many years very happy. The children were happy. The new home was perfect. And there was nothing wrong with the job she had. She and her family had some discerning to do.

"The trick will be," she said, "trying to listen for a word from God, and not just listen to my own desires."

Good luck, I thought.

And I began to wonder, if Larry were her spiritual director, what would he do? Would he point her away from her own distracting, potentially self-serving desires, so she could hear the voice of God, crystal clear, coming from someplace else? Or would he point her to those very desires—potentially twisted, potentially holy—as the place she is most likely to discover the voice of God? Would he say, "God is closer to you than you are to yourself—why don't you start there?"

Not that our desires *are* the voice of God, as if my desiring something is indication enough that God wants me to have it. One look at St. Augustine's life shows that our desires get twisted, and transmuted, and transformed, and we can't trust them at face value all the time. The point is not that our desires are "right," whatever that means, or that they are always ordered and never disordered, or they don't have the possibility to lead us into self-deception. The point is that, however they come to us—ordered or disordered—they are *ours*, so why not listen to them?

This is where a good spiritual director is of immense value, in helping us untangle the holy from the base in our desires, and discerning when following our desires would lead us somehow further into the house of God's love and when following them might be more like running out the back door, the way the prodigal son followed his desire and ran, with his father's money, to a far country.

But remember: he only found his way back to his father's house when he woke up, when, as the Scripture says, "he came to himself." He was able to realize where he belonged when he looked at his life and remembered who he was. And he didn't belong with the swine.

In spiritual direction, as we learn to attend to our lives, and gain some freedom from fretting about the past and preoccupation with the future, freedom to stop and consider the present, we are ever more likely to come to ourselves, remember who we are, and find our way back to our Father's house.

As Robert Benson writes, "The fact that the Voice that calls to us often sounds like our own is not something to be mistrusted or feared. It is a sign of how close God is to us."

———————

Larry helps me in very tangible ways to attend to the shape of my life. He does it by inviting me into a time of silence and then leading me in a meditation. He might invite me to look back over the previous week and to think about things I am grateful for. We are learning together that my natural inclination is not toward gratitude but toward anxiety. I'm often unable to respond in gratitude to the present because I'm preoccupied with anxiety, which seems to live with me sometimes like an uninvited houseguest and won't stop chattering in my ear long enough for me to notice the good and beautiful things right in front of me.

So, even though Larry will lead me in different kinds of meditation, I've noticed that they are most often designed to help me notice those things I have to be grateful for in the present. "And don't just think about things you think you *should* be thankful for, as if there's a right answer," he will say. "Let your mind wander through your life, and let it notice what it hasn't noticed yet."

And then I'll remember—the luscious flavor of the perfectly ripe peach I bought earlier that day at a roadside stand, the fried apple turnovers that two ladies from the church dropped off when I got home from Bible study, the back rub Ginger gave me last night, the page in a book by Frederick Buechner that made me cry but also made me feel more alive than I have in a long time, the moments of quiet that allowed me to read that page, Simeon begging me to wrestle him to the ground and tickle him some more.

Once a month I have a lesson in attending. But attending to our lives once a month is not often enough. For me it's like a reset button. I can be scattered and worn, forgetful and distracted, but that hour every month on Larry's sofa calls me back— from the past that is past and the future that is not here yet, back to the present, where I am and where God is, and where we have the best chance of meeting.

And yet, learning to receive spiritual direction—to attend to our lives as a way of attending to God—doesn't just have to happen in an office or study. What we learn there is portable, so to speak.

And the practice I've discovered, and I would recommend to you, that helps me to be attentive to my life more regularly is a practice I've already mentioned: the daily examen. I've suggested doing a monthly examen as a way of preparing yourself for your meeting with your spiritual director. But the practice is meant to be done every day, and it doesn't take any money or any books, except the book of your life and a pen and journal, if you like to write things down. It's essentially a way of guiding yourself to look at your life prayerfully, the way Larry will often guide me to look at my life.

There are many ways to do it, but here's one suggestion. At the end of your day, find a place where you can be alone and quiet for fifteen minutes. If you have a practice that helps to center you and bring your mind to quiet, do that. Otherwise, light a candle, take a few deep breaths, and repeat a couple of times a familiar verse of Scripture. Take two minutes to do whatever it takes to bring yourself to some measure of quiet. Sometimes for me it's as simple as rubbing my hands on the arms of my chair, as a way of becoming aware of my place, and saying, "Here I am."

And then begin to think about your day, hour by hour. Walk through your day in your mind, asking yourself questions such as these along the way: What do I have to be thankful for today? When today was I rushed, hurried, or distracted? What were my emotions throughout the day—when was I joyful, anxious, sad, happy, despondent, bored, restless? Whom did I see today? Was I able to be present and available to them, or was I distracted and preoccupied? When did I sense God's presence today, or

God's absence? Did I have a chance to respond to God today? When did I have time to breathe? Whose lives did I touch today?

This is also a good time to think about your desires, asking, What did I want today? Did following my wants lead me deeper into God's house, or out the back door? Did following my wants cause me to hurt anyone? Do I need to ask forgiveness?

It's not likely that you'll have answers to all of these questions, or that you'll need to ask them all each night, or that you'll make many extraordinary discoveries. Because most of our lives are pretty mundane. And yet God can speak in and through them anyway.

Mundane or exciting, boring or thrilling, this is the only life you've got, so if you're going to look for any guidance from the Holy Spirit, attending to your own life is the place to start. It's probably the place to finish too.

---

Without asking for it, the door of change was now half-way open. We had a decision to make—open it all the way and walk through, or slam it shut again. When I thought about my children and my wife, I thought, let's fling it open. But when I thought about myself, and my conviction that we should stay longer at our church, and the investment we'd made in getting this fellowship hall built, I wanted to reach out and grab the handle and pull the door shut as fast as I could.

I needed a word. But I didn't want it from Larry this time. I wanted a word from God, and I wanted it to be clear and unambiguous.

We had a week and a half to decide, and I was about to leave for five days on one of my spiritual formation retreats. Surely, if God was going to tell us what to do, that's where God would do it. For five days, I was determined to listen for a word from the Lord. And what a painful five days it was.

I mean painful literally. I had a headache the whole week. It's the headache I call my stress headache. This headache is often my first indicator that I'm under stress and that I'd better stop, figure out what it is, and deal with it. But this time I knew why I had the headache. I didn't know what would get rid of it.

That week I was listening so hard for God, and looking for a sign under every rock, in every gesture, in every word from one of our presenters, that I became more and more confused every day, and more and more frenetic in my search.

Three days into the retreat I found a book in the library by Frederick Buechner, his memoir *Now and Then: A Memoir of Vocation*. As I began reading it, I asked God to use this book to give me a word. As I read about Buechner's discernment about his vocation, maybe God would give me some guidance in my own discernment. In my experience, God doesn't usually agree to these kinds of deals, but it was worth a try.

I came to a crucial place in the book where Buechner describes a decision he had to make: whether to be a minister or a writer. In concrete terms, that meant staying in seminary or quitting to write a book. As I came upon this section, my eagerness for some direction increased. Here, I thought, in his discernment, I will hear from God as well. And what he wrote described exactly how I was feeling and behaving:

> Most of the major decisions of my life I find very hard to remember . . . but I can still remember anguishing my way through this one. I went to Dr. Muilenburg for advice. I consulted my friends. I knew that Christians were

supposed to pray for guidance, and I tried my hand at that, too, in the dark of night, in my bed at 929 Madison Avenue. The anguish was real enough, but I remember that, even at the time, the prayers seemed self-conscious and stagey. I was less a man praying than a man *being* a man praying, and no clear answer came . . .

My pulse quickened as I got to this part, sure that here I would find my word as well. How did God speak to him? How did God guide him? For maybe God would guide me the same way. So I read on.

. . . none that I could hear anyway, and maybe that in itself was the answer: that there was no clear right, no clear wrong, but that whichever way I chose, I would have to make it right, both for me and the one I prayed to.

And my headache got worse as I thought, this isn't good enough. I can't make this decision. But it was the last full day of the retreat, and I hadn't heard a word yet. I was beginning to lose hope.

I had decided I would share this with my covenant group that night. I had been meeting with these same six people for five nights in a row, every three months since the retreats began, so that we might help one another discern God's movement in our lives. We knew each other well, trusted one another, and were getting good at paying attention to one another. They had listened to me every night this week talk about my agony in trying to make a decision. It was the last night, and I was going to tell them I simply had to decide. No word had come.

But before I did, I thought: These people know me, and they've been listening to me, and paying attention to me. Maybe they have been able to see or hear something that I, too anxious and obsessed with hearing from God, have not been able to see or hear. So I invited them to do an exercise. I asked them to take five minutes of silence as we sat together and think about how I had spoken over the week about the decision I needed to make, and how they had experienced me and my longing and desires as long as we had known each other. "And then," I said, "when we're done, I would love for you to share with me what, if anything, came to you in the silence. An image or word, perhaps, that might help me see my own life more clearly."

I was asking them to do for me what I imagined Larry would ask me to do for myself, but what, at that point, I seemed incapable of doing. I couldn't get any perspective on my life at that moment; but I thought these trusted friends might.

And two things happened.

First, during the silence I found myself getting nervous that they might all say, "Roger, we know you, and we believe you need to stay." And this nervousness that they might think I should stay was the first bit of clarity I had about what my own deepest desires might be. And it took silence, and the freedom from my own preoccupation I was given as others carried my burden for a few minutes, that allowed me to catch a glimpse of my desire I wasn't able to catch before.

And the second thing was their responses. Chris simply said, "As you have talked this week, and in weeks past, the only thing I could hear in your voice was a lack—a lack of joy." And Freida said, "This is strange, but I just kept having this image of a warm, roaring fireplace." I wasn't going to try to figure that out.

And then June. June was the visionary in my group. A great listener, she also had a fantastic imagination, and she used that imagination to bless us as she would describe how she prayed for each of us while we were away from one another, imagining us all together playing in her back-yard. I was particularly eager to hear what her imagination came up with.

"I had a picture. Thinking about all you have said, I couldn't help imagining you and Ginger and your boys, sitting in the seat of a Conestoga wagon, driving a team of horses, as you head into an unknown adventure. And I could see the look of excitement on all your faces."

And here's what you're thinking—that was his word. He got what he wanted.

But that's not true. It wasn't what June said that made the difference. I don't know if God gave her that picture or not. What mattered was the way I responded to it. I was joyful when she shared that image. I loved it. I knew, somehow, it was true. And *that* was the word I was looking for— my own reaction. That's how God spoke to me, through my own sense of joy. I suspect if June had said she saw us staying and working for another five years, my heart would have sunk, in which case *that* would have been God's way of speaking. Either way, what this exercise allowed wasn't the chance to receive guidance from God coming from the outside—from others—but the chance to see more clearly my own deepest desires and discover what I really wanted.

My headache went away. I had the first good night's sleep I'd had the whole week. And I drove home the next day knowing that we would be moving soon, not to Charlotte, but to wherever the same bishop who sent us to the country thought Ginger and I could each use our gifts to the fullest.

"Ginger," I said as I walked in the door, "I think we need to start saving boxes, because it's going to be time to pack soon." And I paid attention and saw the biggest smile I'd seen in a long time.

# Go Well

The hour has passed. The conversation is drawing to what feels its natural end. Larry glances to his right, to a small clock positioned on an end table facing him, and he says, "Well, it's time for us to end. Let's look at our calendars for a time next month." He reaches around to his left to get the calendar sitting on his desk. It's that simple. We're done.

But not really.

You might think this calendar-grabbing ritual we perform every month marks an emergence out of the Spirit back into daily life. The holy hour is over. Our calendars symbolize the routine, the ordinary, the mundane that we reenter. We've finished talking about "spiritual things" and normal life has returned—the life of appointments and schedules, of busyness and routine. We've left the spiritual world and entered again the real world.

But that's not what happens at all. Just the opposite happens—we take that whole world, the world we call "real life," into our hands as we grab our calendars, and we pull it into the world of God's Spirit. Taking our calendars in our hands we are saying, I think, *this* is where God is. Not in some holier-than-usual hour, set apart from the rest of life. Rather, this hour is dedicated to helping us stay attentive to the way God's Spirit pervades all of life— the way God is in the appointments, the schedules, the busyness, and the routine, the way God is also in the spaces in between. Between this moment, the end of one hour of spiritual direction, and the date we are about to pick when I will climb into the station wagon once again, toss that apple into the seat beside me, and make the journey to Larry's office next month—those days in between I have the task of living in God's house of love. Those are the days I really get to learn how to long and find, release and offer, trust and attend. What I practice in this hour—receiving spiritual direction—I live the rest of the time, receiving in the daily grind direction from the Spirit of God whom I am learning to notice and love.

Our next meeting time penciled into our calendars, Larry puts on his shoes and walks with me to the door of the office building. We keep chatting as we walk, sometimes about books we're reading, or a recent *Christian Century* article no one else in Franklin County has read.

And here at the door is where he says his final word. If I paid him, this word itself would be worth the cost. If I had received nothing else from our time together—no direction from God through Larry or through the noticing and naming of my own desires, no other word to sustain me, challenge me, or give me hope—this final word would be enough.

Larry shakes my hand, clasping my hand in both of his.

"Take care," I say.

"Go well," he says.

He always says, "Go well."

If you look it up, the first definition of *well* is a noun, the hole you dig in your backyard so that you have water to drink. The next definition is an adverb, meaning "in a good or proper manner." Maybe Larry is telling me, "Go in a good or proper manner."

Some men brought to Jesus a woman who had been caught in the very act of committing adultery. How they managed that, if she wasn't set up, and where her accomplice was do not seem to matter. Whether she was set up or whether her guilt is shared with another, these men don't care. They are using her, perhaps the way other men have used her—having trapped her, they want to use her to trap Jesus.

How will Jesus respond? Will he command what the law commands—stoning? Or is he soft on sin?

But Jesus turned the tables on them. Sure, she can be stoned. But the only one who will be allowed to do it is the one among you without any sin, he says. *I'm waiting. No one? Will no one stone her?*

Jesus doodled in the sand then looked up. Gone—all of her accusers were gone. He was left alone with the woman. "Woman, where are they? Has no one condemned you?"

"No one, sir."

"Neither do I condemn you."

Jesus was a great spiritual director, and good spiritual directors learn from him. He refuses to judge her. Her other accusers have left, and now she is safe. Jesus knows about her dirty laundry—he knows her secret and her shame. But unlike all the others—the man she was sleeping with and the men who used her to trap Jesus—Jesus will not use her. He treats her with integrity. She does not serve any utilitarian purpose for him. She is safe with him.

Good spiritual directors do the same.

But that doesn't mean our spiritual directors will never challenge us, encouraging us to live fully in the newness of life their own compassion has helped us to see that God is offering us, just as Jesus does with the woman: "Go, and sin no more."

Go well, Jesus was saying, using *well*'s adverbial meaning. Go and live *well*. Go and live in the safe space my love has created for you; and in that space, live well, no longer trapped in your own misdirected desires, and no longer trapped by the misdirected desires of others. Go and live in the freedom my refusal to condemn has given you.

He was inviting her to live in the freedom Charles Wesley writes about in the hymn *And Can It Be.*

> Long my imprisoned spirit lay,
> Fast bound in sin and nature's night.
> Thine eye diffused a quick'ning ray;
> I woke; the dungeon flamed with light.
> My chains fell off, my heart was free,
> I rose, went forth, and followed thee.

Those words—*I do not condemn you*—spoken to the woman by Jesus, and spoken to us by Jesus often through others—are the quickening ray, the laser light of love, that breaks the chains that bind us and allows us to hear and respond to Christ's invitation to a different kind of life, a life of increasing freedom to explore our new home in God.

*Go, and sin no more.* Unchained and free-hearted, go well.

―――――

As I chew on the gift of those two simple words, I'm increasingly interested not in the adverbial meaning of *well*, but in its meaning as an adjective: "not ailing, infirm, or diseased; healthy."

Ten lepers approached Jesus. The Bible says they kept their distance. They knew the protocol. They didn't belong anymore. They were unclean. This disease was a sign of God's judgment. They'd been kicked out of God's house, and that meant being kicked out of human society as well. So keeping their distance, they called out to Jesus. "Have mercy on us."

Jesus told them to show themselves to the priest, and as they went they were made clean.

We are used to thinking of this story as a simple healing story. Their bodies were whole again. Their skin was clear. But it also means they belong again. In our culture it's easy to miss the social dimension of this healing. To be made clean means they could come back—they could return to their homes, they could rejoin society, and, most important, they could be welcomed again into God's own house, the temple.

One of the ten lepers stopped before he got to the priest. When he noticed that he was healed—clean—he turned around, ran to Jesus, and, no longer needing to keep his distance, he threw himself at Jesus' feet and thanked him.

Jesus tells him, "Go on your way; your faith has made you well."

Jesus doesn't tell this man to live differently, to live well. He doesn't need to—that's the man's only possibility. Now clean, his life with others and with God has potential he never dreamed he'd have again. Jesus simply tells him that he is well—not ailing, infirm, or diseased, but healthy.

Go well, Larry says, and now I wonder: Is he reminding me of my wholeness in God? Is he telling me to go my way and live in the knowledge that, in God's house, as God's guest, living in God's love, I am whole, healthy, well?

Even though I still experience my own brokenness and sin, I am learning through spiritual direction to hear God's voice reminding me—*in my love you are whole*.

Live in that place, Larry might be saying, in the knowledge of the love of God, who is making you whole. That's a reminder I desperately need.

---

We theologians like to think about something called *eschatology*. Eschatology is the study of the end times, when God will finally bring to a conclusion the story we know as history, when God's plan will be finished. Talking and speculating about eschatology can get pretty heady. But the fourteenth-century English recluse Julian of Norwich sums up the most important point of eschatology beautifully and simply in the words she received from Jesus in a vision: "And all shall be well. And all manner of things shall be well."

In the midst of suffering, evil, and trials of all sorts, Mother Julian is telling us, remember that there is a future as real as the present, because it is God's future, in which all things will be made well.

Spiritual direction helps us to live in that future in the present, to discover when and how that future is making itself visible in our lives.

Can I go, can I leave this office, this holy hour, believing that there is a wellness, a divine cosmic wellness, one that is future and is God's to bring, but that is also as real and present as the Spirit in whom we live and move and have our being? Can I live in that divine wellness? And can you? Can we go well?

Two years ago my gray-haired father, who used to let me stand behind him and comb his wispy hair, standing it up and watching it fall, died. The man who taught me to love going to church and to make a habit of it; who taught me how to be the first in the car on Sunday mornings because whatever I would encounter at church—fellowship with friends, and maybe even with God—was worth being in a hurry for; who taught me how to rub a back, score a baseball game, and tie a tie, was able to teach me one last lesson—how to leave, as he took leave of this life, and I— not by choice—took leave of him and said goodbye.

Dad's dying was between my sessions with Larry, during some of that calendar time I had been learning God inhabits as well as the seemingly holy times. And since I'd been learning to live in God's presence, I was able to see this time as holy time as well.

Dad had pneumonia. It seemed a cruel irony. Dad had always been nervous whenever a cold got into his chest. Nothing made him go to the doctor so fast as a chest cold. He feared it turning to bronchitis and then to pneumonia. I suppose he remembered having pneumonia when he was eighteen, in 1938, before antibiotics. He often told the story of how they put hot mustard plasters on his chest to relieve the congestion. Dad played basketball in high school, and pneumonia benched him for his whole senior season.

And now he had it again. But this time he was eighty-eight. He'd been sick for months—first a cold, then bronchitis. A few rounds of antibiotics failed. When Mom took him back to the doctor and the doctor saw that he was too weak even to walk into the office, the doctor admitted him to the hospital. It was Monday.

On Wednesday afternoon my sister called me. She said my dad, her stepdad, might be put on a respirator that night. He would be put into a medically induced coma. This would give his body a chance to rest while the antibiotics killed the pneumonia. But it might not work. "You better fly home now," she said. "Your dad said he's as scared as he's ever been, and this could be your last chance to talk to him."

I did fly home that night. He hadn't been put on a respirator yet, so my sister picked me and my brother up from the airport late Wednesday night. She drove us home. Mom said Dad was resting, and we could see him in the morning.

These days were a blur. Doctors in and out. Dad, struggling to breathe, the rest of us helplessly staring at the monitors in the room, as if a blip on a screen might give us some kind of hope.

And I did one of the hardest and most necessary things I'd ever done. My mother and brother had gone home, and I stayed to have some time alone with Dad. I am my father's son. Even as a preacher, and even as I had been learning to pray, I am still the son of a midwesterner who never wore his faith on his sleeve. And I don't either. I wanted to ask my dad if I could pray for him. I wanted to open a door with him that had never been opened before. But I was scared. And yet, faced with the possibility that this might be the last chance to open that door, I did what I had wanted to do for years but never knew how—to make my faith a part of our life together as father and son.

"Dad," I said, pulling my chair close to his bed, "can I pray for you?"

"I would welcome that. No one has been to the hospital to pray for me."

So I prayed. I'd done this a million times, it seemed, by the beds of people who expected me to pray. But never with my father, who didn't expect it, but who welcomed it.

And then I asked him if I could sing. There's a Taizé chant I often sing to my boys when they wake up at night with a bad dream and struggle to get back to sleep. I told Dad I wanted to sing that hymn to him, and I did: "Come and fill our hearts with your peace. You alone, O Lord, are holy."

I don't know if God filled his heart with peace. He did have the best night's sleep he'd had in several days. And the last night's sleep he would have without a mask strapped tightly to his face, and medicine calming his anxiety.

The next night, he was asleep before I left. The mask was on him, and the medicine had soothed his nerves enough that he dozed off. He was a little confused because his oxygen level was so low, but before he fell asleep one of the nurses said, "Your son is sitting over there." He looked in my direction and gave me a thumbs-up. That thumbs-up was the last thing he said to me.

And that night I said the last thing I would ever say to him in this life. I didn't know it, although I suspected it. I was flying home the next morning. The doctors were still speaking optimistically, even though nothing was actually improving. Three days later he would be transferred to a hospital in Indianapolis. He would be put on a ventilator.

The infection would spread. His kidneys would fail. And we would wait for a call from Mom that it was time to come home again.

But Dad was sleeping peacefully, a BiPAP machine forcing air into his lungs, his sweaty forehead glistening under the fluorescent lights, his hairline much further back than it was years ago when we played with his hair. I leaned over and kissed his forehead. "I love you," I said. "You're going to be okay."

Of course, I wanted him to be okay in the next few days or weeks. I wanted him to be okay enough to come to North Carolina and see his grandchildren again. That's what I wanted.

But I *knew* he would be okay in the cosmic sense, in the Julian of Norwich sense. He would be well. "All will be well." I knew that not because his doctors were the finest in town, which they were, but because I'd gotten to know the God who makes us well, in whose love we live, whole and loved forever.

As Julian says, "Our soul is made to be God's dwelling place, and the dwelling place of our soul is God who is unmade."

I knew he would be okay because his life was in God's life, whether he knew it or not, although I suspect he did. The house that is God's love would be his home, this night of sleep and forever.

The last thing I said to my dad was a kind of blessing. And I think I was able to say it because for several years I had been learning how to receive blessing. I had been learning how to receive—by longing and finding, by releasing and offering, by trusting and attending—so that now, having received that blessing from Larry every month standing in the door of his office building, I was able to pass that blessing along to my sleeping father.

"You're going to be okay," I said.

In other words, *Go well, Dad, go well.*

———

You and I haven't met. I can't clasp your hand in both of mine or look you in the eye. And I don't know how your spiritual director—if you have one—or any of the soul friends who inhabit life with you and dwell in the house of God's love with you and help you to learn to be attentive to the God who invites you to live and feast in the community of love named Father, Son, and Holy Spirit—those friends who are helping you to recognize your longing for God, who are companioning you as you try to find, who are teaching you how to release, offer, trust, and attend—I don't know how they send you on your way.

There's a lot I don't know, and that means there's a lot I can't do. But I can bless you. As you journey with God, learning to receive guidance from God's Spirit in the exquisite moments and the mundane moments and all the moments in between, I can say to you: Go well, friend, go well.

# acknowledgments

Anyone who has written a book or lived with someone who has written a book, even a short one, knows writing is not a solitary project. I thank my wife, Ginger, for being my best cheerleader. When I thought I would never finish, she said, "You can do it!" And that was just what I needed. She showed patience and flexibility in adjusting our family routines in order to accommodate my writing, and she did it gladly. She was also the first to read the book and gave me valuable input. Thank you, Ginger.

The folks at Paraclete Press deserve my thanks as well, especially for patiently guiding this neophyte author through the publishing maze. Maura Shaw, my editor, saved me from many stylistic infelicities (in other words, from bad writing). She also offered a little spiritual direction along the way. I take full responsibility for any bad writing that remains.

Mostly, I owe my thanks to Larry, but I don't think I need to say why. His influence is on every page of this book, and I hope I have honored the good work that he does.

I dedicate this book to my father, Max Owens. What a wonderful surprise for me, that my search for a spiritual father would lead me to a deeper love and appreciation for my own dad. God is full of surprises, and this was one of his best. I love you and miss you, Dad.

## notes

Author's note: While the stories I have told in this book are true, to the best of my knowledge, I have changed the name of the church and the names and identifying characteristics of members of the church where I was once a pastor in order to protect their privacy.

### introduction My Father's House

xiii  *Sayings of the Desert Fathers*     Benedicta Ward, trans.,
*The Desert Fathers: Sayings of the Early Christian Monks*
(London: Penguin, 2003).

chapter one  **Longing**

8  *Evagrius of Pontus     "If you are a theologian you truly"*
*The Praktikos—Chapters on Prayer,* trans. John Eudes
Bamberger (Spencer, MA: Cistercian, 1970), 65.

9  *With brains in my head and feet in my shoes, as Dr. Seuss*
*put it*     Dr. Seuss, *Oh, the Places You'll Go!* (New York:
Random House, 1990), 2.

11  *"Try to find out what"*     Ephesians 5:10.

*"So do not be foolish"*     Ephesians 5:17.

*"pray without ceasing, give thanks"*     1 Thessalonians
5:17–18.

*"discern what is the will of the Lord"*     Romans 12:2.

*"present your bodies as a living sacrifice"*     Romans 12:1.

*"be perfect"*     Matthew 5:48.

20  *Jason Byassee writes . . .  "Prayer is ultimately"*     Jason Byassee, *The Gifts of the Small Church* (Nashville:
Abingdon, 2010), 30.

chapter two  Finding

33  *As Thomas Merton said, "Spiritual direction"*   Thomas
Merton, *Contemplation* (New York: Herder and Herder,
1969), 41.

*As Jonathan Wilson-Hartgrove has written, "Like wood-
working"*     Jonathan Wilson-Hartgrove, *The Wisdom
of Stability: Rooting Faith in a Mobile Culture* (Brewster,
MA: Paraclete Press, 2010), 60.

34  *Moses replied, "Go and sit"*    Ward, *The Desert Fathers*,
10.

35  *"Anyone without a soul-friend"*      Quoted in Kenneth
Leech, *Soul Friend: Spiritual Direction in the Modern
World* (Harrisburg, PA: Morehouse, 2001), 45.

37  *in the words of Kenneth Leech, . . . "foundation for the
development"*    Leech, *Soul Friend*, 54.

43  *The Westminster Shorter Catechism . . . "What is the chief "*
*The Confession of Faith of the Presbyterian Church in
the United States together with the Larger and the Shorter Catechism* (Atlanta: John Knox Press, 1965), 287.

chapter three  Releasing

49  *poet Denise Levertov writes . . .  "no effort earns"*
Denise Levertov, "The Avowal," *The Stream and the
Sapphire* (New York: New Direction, 1997), 6.

52  *"Those who want to save"*      Mark 8:35.

53   *I love the story of the Desert Father*    Ward, *The Desert Fathers*, 172–173.

56   *Rowan Williams calls "self-dramatizing and fantasy"* Rowan Williams, *Where God Happens: Discovering Christ in One Another* (Boston: New Seeds, 2005), 95.

60   *Stories like this one: A hermit said, "Someone"*    Ward, *The Desert Fathers*, 47.

62   *St. Benedict . . . began with obedience: Listen carefully* St. Benedict, *The Rule of Saint Benedict*, ed. Timothy Fry (New York: Vintage, 1981), 3.

63   *Elizabeth Canham has said: The kind of listening* Elizabeth Canham, *Heart Whispers: Benedictine Wisdom for Today* (Nashville: Upper Room, 1999), 141.

64   *F. W. Faber warned, "The souls"*    Quoted in Leech, *Soul Friend*, 66.

66   *"Dreams of fame and fortune . . ." writes Frederick Buechner*    Frederick Buecher, *Now and Then: A Memoir of Vocation* (New York: HarperCollins, 1983), 31.

69   *Thomas Kelly . . . "We are torn loose"*    Thomas R. Kelly, *A Testament of Devotion* (New York: Harper and Brothers, 1941), 41.

### chapter four  Offering

79  *The presenter talked about*    The presenter was Robert Benson.

86  *Margaret Guenther . . . . She says that*    Margaret Guenther, *Holy Listening: The Art of Spiritual Direction* (Lanham, MD: Cowley, 1992), 26–27.

87  *Parker Palmer calls a "circle of trust"*    Parker J. Palmer, *A Hidden Wholeness: The Journey Toward an Undivided Life* (San Francisco: Jossey-Bass, 2004), 51–87.

88  *the Psalm says, "Who may abide"*    Psalm 15:1–2.

90  *The early Desert Fathers warned*    Ward, *The Desert Fathers*, 23.

### chapter five  Trusting

98  *Paula D'Arcy . . . "God comes to you"*    Quoted in Richard Rohr, "Epiphany: You Can't Go Home Again," St. Anthony Messenger, accessed Sept. 6, 2011, http://www.americancatholic.org/messenger/jan2001/feature3.asp.

109  *Anthony the Great replied, "Wherever you go"*    Ward, *The Desert Fathers*, 3.

112  *God said: Let there be light*    *Upper Room Worshipbook*, ed. Elise Eslinger (Nashville: Upper Room, 2006), 8.

113 *"Early on the first day of the week"*      John 20:1.

 *Parker Palmer calls "functional atheism"*      Parker J. Palmer, *Let Your Life Speak: Listening for the Voice of Vocation* (San Francisco: Jossey-Bass, 2000), 88.

115 *"though we stumble"*      Psalm 37:24.

116 *"Who shall ascend the hill"*      Psalm 24:3–4.

chapter six      **Attending**

121 *As one of those desert monks said, "If someone"*      Ward, *The Desert Fathers*, 109.

126 *Henri Nouwen suggests . . . "Our individual as well"* Henri Nouwen, *Making All Things New: An Invitation to the Spiritual Life* (New York: HarperCollins, 1981), 26–27.

127 *"I tell you, do not worry"*      Matthew 6:25–26, 28.

130 *For, as he discovered, God was closer to him*      Augustine expresses the nearness of the God for whom he was searching in his *Confessions* 3.6. See *The Confessions of St. Augustine,* trans. Hal Helms (Brewster, MA: Paraclete Press, 1986), 46.

133 *"he came to himself"*      Luke 15:17.

 *As Robert Benson writes, "The fact that"*      Robert Benson, *The Echo Within* (Colorado Springs, CO: WaterBrook, 2009), 17.

139 *As I read about Buechner's discernment* . . . *: Most of
    the major decisions* . . . *none that I could hear anyway"*
    Buechner, *Now and Then*, 32.


                                      conclusion   **Go Well**

148 *Some men brought to Jesus a woman*     John 8:1-11.

150 *Charles Wesley.* . . . *Long my imprisoned*     *The Works of
    John Wesley: Volume 7: A Collection of Hymns for the Use
    of the People Called Methodists*, ed. Franz Hildebrandt
    and Oliver Beckerlegge (Nashville: Abingdon, 1983),
    323.

151 *Ten lepers approached Jesus. The Bible says*     Luke
    17:11–19.

153 Julian of Norwich sums up . . . : And all shall be well
    Julian of Norwich, *Showings of Love*, trans. Julia Bolton
    Holloway (Collegeville, MN: Liturgical Press), ch. 27, 37.

157 *Taizé chant* . . . *"Come and fill our hearts"*     *Songs of
    Prayer from Taizé* (Chicago: GIA Publications, 1991),
    49.

158 *As Julian says, "Our soul"*     *Showings of Love*, ch. 54,
    81.

If you would like to read more about the practice of spiritual direction, a great place to begin is chapter 6, "Companions on the Journey: The Gift of Spiritual Direction," in Marjorie Thompson's *Soul Feast: An Invitation to the Christian Spiritual Life* (Louisville: Westminster John Knox, 1995). This chapter is an excellent, short introduction. For a longer and more detailed history of the practice read Kenneth Leech's *Soul Friend: Spiritual Direction in the Modern World* (Harrisburg, PA: Morehouse, 2001). His chapter on the relationship between spiritual direction, counseling, and therapy (chapter 3) is particularly helpful. I have also found the book *Spiritual Direction: Wisdom for the Long Walk of Faith* (New York: HarperCollins, 2006) by Henri Nouwen, with Michael J. Christensen and Rebecca J. Laird, to be helpful in naming some of the important questions we ask in spiritual direction. Rebecca Laird has also written an appendix to the book, called "How to Find a Spiritual Director." Finally, if you want to know what a spiritual director is doing when he or she gives spiritual direction, read Margaret Guenther's *Holy Listening: The Art of Spiritual Direction* (Lanham, MD: Cowley, 1992). While it's written for people who are or want to become spiritual directors, it's very accessible for anyone who wants to gain an inside look at what a spiritual director is doing.

The notes in these books will take you to hundreds of others. Happy reading!

# About Paraclete Press

## Who We Are

Paraclete Press is a publisher of books, recordings, and DVDs on Christian spirituality. Our publishing represents a full expression of Christian belief and practice—from Catholic to Evangelical, from Protestant to Orthodox.

We are the publishing arm of the Community of Jesus, an ecumenical monastic community in the Benedictine tradition. As such, we are uniquely positioned in the marketplace without connection to a large corporation and with informal relationships to many branches and denominations of faith.

## What We Are Doing

### Books

Paraclete publishes books that show the richness and depth of what it means to be Christian. Although Benedictine spirituality is at the heart of all that we do, we publish books that reflect the Christian experience across many cultures, time periods, and houses of worship. We publish books that nourish the vibrant life of the church and its people—books about spiritual practice, formation, history, ideas, and customs.

We have several different series, including the best-selling Paraclete Essentials and Paraclete Giants series of classic texts in contemporary English; A Voice from the Monastery—men and women monastics writing about living a spiritual life today; award-winning literary faith fiction and poetry; and the Active Prayer Series that brings creativity and liveliness to any life of prayer.

### Recordings

From Gregorian chant to contemporary American choral works, our music recordings celebrate sacred choral music through the centuries. Paraclete distributes the recordings of the internationally acclaimed choir Gloriæ Dei Cantores, praised for their "rapt and fathomless spiritual intensity" by *American Record Guide,* and the Gloriæ Dei Cantores Schola, which specializes in the study and performance of Gregorian chant. Paraclete is also the exclusive North American distributor of the recordings of the Monastic Choir of St. Peter's Abbey in Solesmes, France, long considered to be a leading authority on Gregorian chant.

### DVDs

Our DVDs offer spiritual help, healing, and biblical guidance for life issues: grief and loss, marriage, forgiveness, anger management, facing death, and spiritual formation.

Learn more about us at our website:
www.paracletepress.com, or call us toll-free at 1-800-451-5006.

# Discover the "Active Prayer Series"

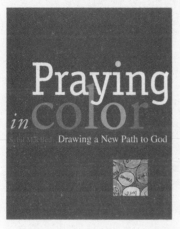

## Praying in Color
*Drawing a New Path to God*

Sybil MacBeth

ISBN: 978-1-55725-512-9
$16.95, Paperback

For the word-weary, stillness-challenged, easily distracted pray-er.

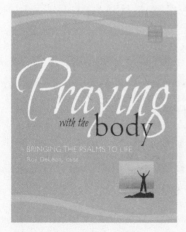

## Praying with the Body
*Bringing the Psalms to Life*

Roy De Leon

ISBN: 978-1-55725-589-1
$16.99, Paperback

This book is an invitation to move in prayer by expressing the psalms with motion.

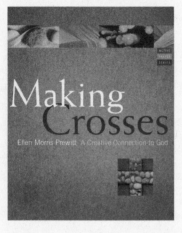
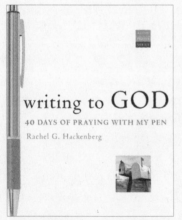